More Spots from the Leopard

More Spots from the Leopard

Fenton Wyness

Impulse Books

Aberdeen 1973

First published in 1973 by

IMPULSE PUBLICATIONS LIMITED

28 Guild Street

Aberdeen

Scotland

ISBN 901311 43 X

For

FRED

Kyle of Tongue

1973

PRINTED BY HINDSON PRINT GROUP LTD

NEWCASTLE UPON TYNE

Acknowledgements

The author desires to express his grateful thanks to the undernoted for their assistance in connection with the writing of this book:

> John H. S. Gordon of Abergeldie.
> Captain Robin de La Lanne Mirrlees, London.
> John Lamb Esq., A.R.I.B.A., A.R.I.C.S.
> E. A. Carson, Librarian, H. M. Customs & Excise, London.
> D. McLachlan Esq., H. M. Customs & Excise.
> W. Welch Esq., H. M. Customs & Excise.
> Edward S. Massie Esq.
> Frederick G. P. Casely Esq. St.J., F.S.A.Scot.
> Norman G. Mar Esq., S.B.St.J., A.R.I.B.A.
> Department of the Environment, Angusfield, Aberdeen.
> Aberdeen University (Anatomy Department).
> Corporation of the City of Aberdeen (Town Clerk's Department).
> Aberdeen Public Library (Miss M. Wilkie, A.L.A. and Staff of the Reference and Local Departments).

and to the following for illustrations:

> Edward S. Massie Esq.
> Frederick G. P. Casely Esq., St.J., F.S.A.Scot.
> Duncan Glennie Esq.
> The National Museum of Antiquities.
> Department of the Environment.

Contents

Illustrations

Introduction

More Spots from the Leopard may be called the sequel to a book I wrote in 1970—*Spots from the Leopard*—which had its measure of popularity.

The stories included here deal with a variety of subjects—people, places and unsolved mysteries—and cover that area known as Scotland's north-east corner.

In writing this book, I have enjoyed the interest and help of a great many people to whom I offer my sincere thanks. I also wish to acknowledge the part played by the Publishers whose co-operation has made the production possible.

Fenton Wyness

45 Salisbury Terrace,
Aberdeen

15th August, 1973

PROLOGUE

We'll Meet Again

"Memory gild the past"—T. Moore.

We often hear the phrase 'Should a doctor tell?'—a query which could well be applied generally for nearly everybody, at one time or another, has been faced with the dilemma—should I tell what I know or keep silent?

Many years ago, a client of mine picked up an old chair—an interesting 16th-century arm chair with turned front supports, sloping arms and a carved panel at the back. He paid £5 for it—'a genuine bargain in bog-oak'—or so the second-hand dealer told him. This was my introduction to 'The Chair'.

One day in summer, about eighteen months later, my client discovered to his horror a sporadic outbreak of worm-holes spreading from the carved panel of the chair. He had some unusually fine pieces of furniture in his beautiful home and lest any of these should become affected, he threw the chair out. In his own words he "had no faith in the new-fangled woodworm stuff". Accordingly, the chair was broken up and the panel burned—but my Aberdonian instincts prompted me to collect the pieces.

Some months later, I began treating the several pieces and eventually put them together again. However, in the process I had learned something interesting—the 'bog-oak' proved to be several layers of black paint! 'The Chair' was of light-coloured birch. A sculptor friend carved a new panel for the back and the transformed chair again went into circulation.

Alas, before very long, the worms again took over. This time. 'The Chair' went to the saleroom where it fetched £1·50. I thought I had seen the last of it—but here I was wrong.

Time passed and about two years later a local antique dealer telephoned to ask if I would be interested to see a very fine piece he had just acquired—"historically unique" he called it for "it belonged to the famous Wizard Laird of Skene". As it happened, I was at the time going into the history of this fantastic Aberdeenshire character and went to see the dealer. However, I was not prepared for the shock I received on entering his showroom—it was 'The Chair'. It had undergone another metamorphosis—'bog-oak' again while the value had rocketed to £20. There was no sale, at least not to me, but I wondered—should a person tell?

Nearly two years elapsed then, one evening, I was astonished to see my old friend in a new role—on the stage in a period play where 'The Chair' made an impressive 'prop'. The credit in the programme informed the audience it had been kindly lent by "Lady X in whose family it had been for generations". With the final curtain, I felt sure I had seen it for the last time—once again I was wrong.

Another year passed and one Saturday afternoon, finding myself a member of a party in a conducted tour round one of the stately homes in the county, I listened to the female guide recounting everything we should know about the family and their manorial seat. Every portrait, knick-nack and piece of furniture had its story recounted with commendable brevity—other customers were waiting! But when we came to the *piece de resistance*, only then did our guide slow down, lingering, lovingly over it—a family treasure cherished down the centuries. Yes, indeed, it was 'The Chair'.

Should a person tell?—or do as I did—recall the words of the well-known song—

> *"We'll meet again, don't know where, don't know when"*

1

The Witch of Abergeldie

"Ran-tree and reid threed
Pits the witches to their speed."—Traditional.

Abergeldie Castle, on the south bank of the Aberdeenshire Dee about six miles above Ballater, is one of the best-known houses in the country, for its long association with the British Royal Family has brought it world-wide publicity. Adjoining the Balmoral Estates, Abergeldie Castle has, since Queen Victoria's time, figured annually in Court Circulars during the Scottish Season and the comings and goings of Royalty and their guests would seem to have added lustre to the ancient tower-house.

Abergeldie, which came into the possession of the Gordons in 1478, is one of the few Aberdeenshire properties remaining in the possession of the original family settled there, the present owner, John Howard Seton Gordon being 21st laird of Abergeldie. As one would expect, the castle is particularly rich in history and legendary lore but among the plethora of shadowy figures from the past there predominates one astonishing character—the nebulous Kitty Rankine, witch of Abergeldie.

It was during the lairdship of Alexander Gordon, 4th of Abergeldie, that James VI (1567–1625) issued the most remarkable document of his reign. Dated 2nd February, 1596, and given under his hand from "Haliruid-hous", this was his *Commission in favour of the Provost and Baillies of the Burgh of Aberdeen* authorising them to hold Justice Courts in an attempt to eradicate the "detestabill practizeis of witchcraft and sorcerie". The Provost—Alexander Chalmers of Cults—and indeed the whole Town Council would appear to have taken up the royal witch-hunt with almost indecent zest as indicated by the astonishing documentary evidence preserved in the city's archives. However, before the king's *Commission* was implemented, Alexander Gordon died and it was his son Alexander, 5th of Abergeldie, who became involved in the subsequent Trials for Witchcraft.

As one would expect during such a fantastic period in history, both fact and fiction combined in recording events consequently, after a lapse of over three centuries, it would seem that fiction triumphed in the oft-repeated tale of Abergeldie's personal witch Kitty Rankine.

Basically, the Abergeldie district possesses all the necessary ingredients for a Black Magic story. Covens of witches actually existed and were active in the neighbourhood, indeed the names of their members are on record. In addition, there are several places known to be closely associated with the pagan fertility rites observed by the witches—Ullachie Loch (loch-of-preparing), Creag-nam-ban (hill-of-the-women) and of course the numerous stone circles in the locality. There are, too, the Gallow Hill and the Chapel of St Colm with its surrounding graveyard—both essential to the practice of the Black Arts. With this fertile background, the Kitty Rankine story originated, but the question arises—was it fact or fiction?

It would seem the story started during, or shortly after, the lifetime of Alexander Gordon, 5th of Abergeldie, who succeeded his father in 1596 and died in 1601. At this time, the fear of witchcraft was at its height while the Reformed Church of Scotland, backed by King James, was at its most active in eradicating the 'devilishe sorceries' of the witches. It was regarded as the church's duty to 'seike out' and bring before the local Presbytery anyone suspected of dealing in the Black Arts—a duty which unfortunately afforded considerable scope to the less scrupulous. Consequently, nobody was safe whatever their station in life.

In 1586, Alexander Gordon, the 5th laird, married Margaret, daughter of William Mackintosh of that ilk, widow of the laird of Grant and of the laird of Pitsligo. Gordon was a staunch Roman Catholic and, as the Reformation served only to intensify his fervour for the ancient faith, he was immediately suspect. In his youth, he had fathered a natural son—his only child—referred to in local records as Alexander Gordon "in Aberarder". These three facts would appear to be the kernel of the legend.

Dealing first with fiction. Tradition asserts that the illigitimate Alexander Gordon married one, Catherine Frankie (Gaelic: *Caitir Fhrangach*)—alias 'French Kate' or Kitty Rankine—personal maid to Margaret Mackintosh, the 5th laird's wife. Kitty Rankine—in old Scots 'kitty' denotes a loose woman which may be significant in the story—was a reputed witch. The legend tells that once, when the laird of Abergeldie was returning from a trip to the continent, his lady, knowing of her maid's occult powers, asked her to find out how the laird was occupying his time aboard ship. Anxious to please her mistress, Kitty locked herself into her 'garret' in the castle and, 'working her woe', divined that Abergeldie was enjoying himself immensely in doubtful female company. This information Kitty reported to her mistress whose jealous, quick temper was immediately aroused and she ordered her maid to have the revelry stopped forthwith. Again Kitty retired to her 'garret' and putting everything she knew into her spell, raised a great storm at sea. So successful was her effort that the vessel was wrecked—some versions of the tale saying "with the loss of all on board". At all events, it seems the lady of Abergeldie denounced her maid as a practising witch and the hapless Kitty was thrown into the castle's 'pit' to await trial. Eventually, Kitty Rankine was brought before the barony court at

Abergeldie, found guilty of witchcraft and condemned to death by burning. The gruesome sentence was subsequently carried out on the slopes of Creag-nam-ban where, tradition tells, her pitiful cries may still be heard on the anniversary of the tragic event. From the foregoing story, there are a number of points which obviously cannot be confirmed or explained so that one is left speculating—did Kitty Rankine ever exist?

Passing now to fact. In the records of the *Trials for Witchcraft* preserved in the archives of the city of Aberdeen, the name Kitty Rankine does not appear nor is she listed as being a member of any of the covens active in Aberdeenshire. However, the name of Alexander Gordon, 5th of Abergeldie, is noted in the *Precepts by the Commissioners appointed for the Trials of Witches*. Dated "the sext day of Appryill 1597", this document authorises John Thayne, Messenger to the Commissioners, to charge a number of Aberdeenshire "Lairdis" to "tak and apprehend" certain persons in their locality suspected of Witchcraft and "keip them in firmance" until 23rd April, on which date they should be delivered to the King's Commissioners for trial in Aberdeen. Abergeldie is one of the "Lairdis" mentioned.

Who was the person for whose apprehension Alexander Gordon is charged? Her name is given as Jonet Guisset (Janet Wishart), spouse to John Leys, stabler in the Schoolhill, Aberdeen. Actually, both Janet and her husband were natives of the parish of Crathie and it may be assumed that, on the first murmurings of a witch-hunt within the burgh of Aberdeen, Janet fled to Crathie where in the remote countryside and among her own people, she might stand a better chance of avoiding arrest. However, as Janet Wishart appeared before the Assizes at Aberdeen on 23rd April, 1597, presumably she was taken by the laird of Abergeldie and kept 'in firmance' in the castle 'pit' until delivered to the King's Commissioners for trial. On 18 points of 31 charges, Janet was found guilty of witchcraft and condemned to death by burning. Her son Thomas Leys—also accused of dealing in the Black Arts—was condemned and burnt, both on the Heading Hill at Aberdeen. Her three daughters Elspet, Janet and Violet were banished for life.

Comparing the legend of Kitty Rankine with the authenticated case of Janet Wishart, it is obvious that in a number of details the two run parallel. The latter was seemingly the basis for the former and the fictitious Kitty Rankine was none other than Janet Wishart. The Kitty Rankine story first appeared in print in 1861 when John Grant's *Legends of the Braes o' Mar* was published. He was a native of the region and familiar with all the folk-tales and history of upper Deeside. Grant liked a good story and recounted these in his *Legends* with considerable zest and charm. So the tale of Kitty Rankine and her nebulous links with Abergeldie Castle became known to a very wide public—indeed the hapless creature eventually found her way into *A King's Story*, the Memoirs of H.R.H. The Duke of Windsor.

2

A Family of Miniature Painters

*"Genius does what it must, and Talent
does what it can."*—Owen Meredith.

In the history of Aberdeenshire, it is remarkable how often the
spark of genius touches some ordinary family, is fanned by circumstances and eventually bursts into flame to illuminate
posterity. One of the most fascinating examples of this phenom-
enon is the Robertson family of Cluny who laboured on the
land until one day the spark of genius touched them.

For upwards of two centuries, the Robertsons were tenant
farmers of Drumnahoy in the Aberdeenshire parish of
Cluny—they settled there from Perthshire and were said to be
descended from 'Stalwart John' Robertson of Kindeace, a
cadet of the Struan family. The first of the Drumnahoy
Robertsons to be noted is David, whose elder brother John was
parish minister of Cluny from around 1580–1617. David is
believed to have been born about the year 1590 and lived to
the great age of one hundred and eleven. He was succeeded by
his eldest son John, born in 1635. John Robertson had two
sons, James (1671–1735) and Andrew, the former following
his father as tenant of Drumnahoy—they are mentioned in the
List of pollable persons within the Shire of Aberdeen (1696).

James Robertson married Jean Reid, Kemnay, and by her
had three sons and four daughters. Their eldest son James
(1702–1735), who succeeded to Drumnahoy, married a neighbouring farmer's daughter, Elizabeth Milne of Clack, and they
had a family of two—William (1732–1817) and Jean, both
born at Drumnahoy. On James Robertson's death in 1735,

Elspeth Milne moved to Aberdeen with her young family while Drumnahoy was taken over by James's younger brother Andrew, formerly tenant of Nether Drumnahoy—thus the Robertsons' association with the Cluny district continued.

However, at this point destiny stepped in when the direct line of Drumnahoy Robertsons left the land and turned to the Arts, for in Aberdeen, William Robertson became an architectural draughtsman. In 1764 he married Jean Ross (1738–1811), daughter of Alexander Ross, farmer, of Balnagowan, Monymusk, by whom he had a family of six—four sons and two daughters, three of the sons becoming artists—miniature-painters—of international reputation. William Robertson was a skilled draughtsman but steady employment in this line was difficult to find in Aberdeen. To supplement his income he designed and carved small pieces of furniture but unhappily his meagre earnings failed to meet the family budget—a son and a daughter were in delicate health—and he was obliged to find employment in Edinburgh. Even here the work was not sufficiently remunerative to support the family in Aberdeen and the major burden of providing for their needs fell to his wife Jean Ross, a woman of fine character and infinite resource.

The eldest of the Robertsons' family was Archibald, born at Balnagowan, Monymusk, on 8th May, 1765. He received his early education in Aberdeen and subsequently attended classes at King's College, Old Aberdeen. However, Art was his real interest—a lone furrow to plough in a city where the accumulation of 'siller' is the hall-mark of success. At the age of seventeen, Archibald went to Edinburgh to study water-colour painting and oils but how the family resources were able to sustain his training period is a matter of speculation.

At this time there were in Aberdeen a number of wealthy men—patrons of the Arts—who when they found a young man of talent but without the necessary means to further his career, generously saw them through a recognised course of training either in Edinburgh or London. One of these men was John Ewen, a prosperous goldsmith and jeweller in the Castlegate, who not only possessed a fine collection of pictures including works by Hemskerck, Holbien, Rembrant, Rubens, Titian, Vandyck and Zoffany, but was personally acquainted with all the notable artists of the day. John Ewen knew the Robertson family—he sponsored the training of Andrew, the youngest of the three artist brothers—and it is possible he may have assisted Archibald and Alexander.

At this time, his father's health was beginning to fail and in 1784 Archibald returned to Aberdeen where he taught for a time, his two most promising pupils being his younger brothers Alexander and Andrew.

In 1786 he went to London attending the Royal Academy Schools and studying miniature-painting under Charles Shirreffs of Bath. The turning point in Archibald Robertson's career came in 1791 when he went to New York carrying with him a letter of introduction from David, 11th Earl of Buchan, to the President of the United States of America—George Washington. He was cordially received by Washington and painted miniatures of the President, his wife and family. Archibald Robertson decided to remain in New York. Here he planned and opened the Columbian Academy of Fine Arts and eventually was appointed Director of the American Academy of Arts. He was the author of a treatise on miniature-painting and devices in hair work for lockets—an art then at the height of its popularity. Archibald Robertson married Eliza Abramse of New York by whom he had a large family. Failing eyesight put an end to his career and he died in New York in 1835.

The second and third members of the Robertson family were a daughter, blind from infancy due to smallpox, and a mentally retarded son.

The fourth member of the family was Alexander, born in Aberdeen on 13th May, 1772. From an early age he showed much promise in Art and from his eldest brother Archibald received his initial training. In 1791 he went to London where he studied at the Royal Academy Schools and with Samuel Shelly the miniature-painter. The following year he went to New York joining his brother Archibald in his Columbian Academy project. Alexander next moved to Canada—in 1799—where the scenery delighted him and he painted a great deal. However, his ability and popularity as a teacher was such that after 1802 he produced very little work yet, from 1817 onwards, he exhibited regularly at the American Academy. He played a major part in developing art education in the public schools of New York, and in 1820 was appointed Keeper of the American Academy.

Alexander Robertson married Mary, daughter of Bishop Provost, by whom he had a large family. He died in New York in 1841.

The fifth and perhaps the most talented of the Robertson family was Andrew, born in Aberdeen on 14th October, 1777. Although early in life he showed some interest in Art, at the age of fifteen he entered Marischal College, Aberdeen, with the idea of following a medical career. However, for some obscure reason—probably the lack of the necessary means—he began painting anything from stage scenery to flags and banners for parades. It was during this difficult period in his career that the already-mentioned John Ewen took a practical interest in the struggling young artist. He provided the necessary funds for Andrew's proper training in Edinburgh and gave him letters of introduction to various famous artists including Sir Henry Raeburn and Alexander Nasmyth, both of whom opened their studios to him.

Back in Aberdeen in 1794, he was appointed art master at Robert Gordon's Hospital. Much of his time was spent in painting miniatures but by working sixteen hours a day, he somehow managed to study, taking his M.A. at Marischal College.

Although by this time Andrew Robertson was becoming well-known in north-east Scotland, he decided he must move to London if he was to further his career. Accordingly, in 1801, he entered the Royal Academy Schools, and with letters of introduction from his benefactor John Ewen, was cordially received in many of the famous studios of the day. The following year he exhibited at the Royal Academy for the first time—a miniature self-portrait.

In 1803, Andrew Robertson returned to Aberdeen to paint several miniatures including one of his friend Ewen. The threatened invasion of Great Britain by Napoleon was at this time causing much anxiety especially along the east coast. Robertson joined the local Volunteers—he was a fine bugler—and subsequently was promoted Lieutenant.

Back in London in 1805 and with his appointment as Miniature-Painter to H.M. The Duke of Sussex, his career was now assured. Three years later he exhibited at the Royal Academy miniature-portraits of five Princesses and other royal commissions followed.

Andrew Robertson was twice married. By his first wife—known to posterity as 'Jenny', he had two sons, Edward (1809–1831) who followed the family tradition in Art and became a miniature-painter, and Charles. Andrew's second wife was a daughter of Samuel Boxhill of Barbados by whom he had Samuel and Emily who in 1895 edited her father's *Letters and Papers of Andrew Robertson*. His last public appearance was in 1841 when he attended a Levee held by the young Queen Victoria—an outstanding figure in his full Highland dress. The same year Andrew visited Aberdeen but his health was failing—he had painted over a thousand miniature-portraits—and he died at his home in Hampstead, London, on 5th December, 1845.

The sixth and youngest member of the Robertson family was a daughter—an invalid from birth. The story of the

Robertsons of Drumnahoy and Aberdeen is indeed a strange one—three of its members endowed with genius and vigour while three were burdened by ill health—mental and physical.

But "genius does what it must"; Archibald and Alexander carried their talent to America where their influence on the Art of that country endures, while Andrew made a unique contribution to miniature-painting in Great Britain. Many of his works can be seen in public galleries, others are in private hands, but the finest of his miniatures are in the royal collection of H.M. The Queen.

3

St Catherine's Dub

"Ships that pass in the night."—Longfellow.

From time immemorial, the wild and rocky Buchan coast of Aberdeenshire has been the 'graveyard' of countless ships—many of them nameless. Driven to destruction by gales, fogs or heavy seas, there must indeed be few rock-bound recesses along the shore but has its quota of wrecks and even today fragments of forgotten ships are cast ashore.

On studying the Ordnance Survey Maps of the Buchan coast, one is immediately struck by the remarkable variety of fascinating place-names for almost every outstanding feature along this rugged shore is labelled. The usual reaction is to speculate as to the origins of these picturesque names which, from earliest times have been passed on verbally by generation after generation until finally recorded by the Government surveyors in 1867.

The names appear to be derived from three main sources—Gaelic, Norse and what what might be called 'Local'. Naturally, with the passage of time, there are a number of obvious corruptions whose origins are obscure and one can only hazard a guess as to their meaning.

One of these mystery names is *St Catherine's Dub*—a deep pool in a V-shaped creek just north of the village of Collieston—about which the Ordnance Survey Maps add the rider "Site of the wreck of the St Catherine, one of the Ships of the Spanish Armada A.D. 1588." This clear-cut statement cannot fail to arouse interest and kindle the desire to learn more about the St Catherine and of its fate on the rocky Aberdeen-shire coast. Assuming St Catherine's Dub to be a 'Local' place-name, presumably the Government surveyors must have obtained their information on the spot, accepted it as being authentic and subsequently published it in good faith.

In 1840, Lieutenant Paterson R.N. of the local Coastguard Station, discovered at low tide in a creek just north of Collieston village, what appeared to be two guns and a sea-chest. During the summer of that year, he was successful in raising one of the guns, much corroded and broken off near the muzzle. A sketch of this weapon subsequently appeared in *The Illustrated London News* and created widespread interest.

Fifteen years later—in the autumn of 1855—the Rev James Rust, parish minister of Slains, succeeded in raising another gun from the same pool. This was of malleable iron 7 ft. 9 in. in length with $\frac{3}{4}$ in. bore, the 4 lb. ball and wadding being intact and in surprisingly good condition. This gun is preserved at Haddo House, Aberdeenshire. In May, 1876, the Countess of Erroll employed a diving party to search the same creek and was successful in salvaging two guns and an anchor—now pre-served at Old Slains—while in August, 1880, the largest and most complete gun in malleable iron was raised from the same site. Measuring 8ft. in length and with a 4 in. diameter bore, the ball and wadding were again intact and in a good state of preservation. It eventually found its way to London.

Nearly a century later—in 1970—the Peterhead Dolphin Diving Club, in collaboration with Dr Andrew Shivas, Edinburgh, renewed investigations on the same site—this time with modern skin-diving equipment. Tides were difficult and visibility poor, yet they were successful in recovering a gun and an anchor.

It would seem that none of the objects recovered from the sea-bed here have been categorically identified as being of Spanish origin—indeed the only authentic Spanish relics found in the neighbourhood appear to be eight silver coins, one dated 1555, picked up from the land by Robert Clark, feuar and farmer, Collieston. How then did the story of the wreck of the Spanish ship St Catherine originate?

Details of the Spanish Armada are matters of history and as many important books have been written on the subject repetition is unnecessary—except where it touches on the quest for information regarding the origin of the name *St Catherine's Dub.*

Dealing first with the Armada, the Spanish Fleet consisted of 130 ships—the joint Armadas of Andalusia, Biscay, Castile, Guipuzcoa, Levant and Portugal together with storeships, transports, light craft, galleasses and galleys. The name of every vessel is recorded together with its tonnage, number of guns and compliment of troops and sailors. The list reveals that none of the ships bore the name St Catherine (*Santa Catarina*). However, three ships named *Santa Catalina* are noted—the first belonging to Andalusia, a galleon of 730 tons with 23 guns; the second to Castile, a galleon of 882 tons with 24 guns; and the third a light craft (tender) without guns. Could there have been confusion between the names *Catarina* and *Catalina*? This is unlikely for, dismissing the third *Santa Catalina*—the light craft without guns—as being irrelevant, the two damaged galleons of the same name succeeded in limping back to the same port of Santander.

Dealing next with circumstances. It is recorded that, when the English Fleet finally abandoned the pursuit of the crippled Armada in the North Sea opposite the Firth of Forth, the Spaniards took the opportunity of reviewing the damage done to their ships. This inspection took place about a hundred miles off the east coast of Scotland. A strong, south-west gale was then blowing—as a contemporary weather report states "squalls, rain and fog with heavy sea". It was impossible, therefore, for any of the Spanish galleons to have been driven towards the rock-bound coast of Buchan and indeed if any alien ship had been driven ashore at such a time of national tension, detailed information of the incident would most certainly have been transmitted to Edinburgh without delay. As it was, only four wrecks of Spanish vessels were recorded in Scottish waters—at Fair-Isle, Salen, Lochaline and Tobermory.

Passing finally to local knowledge of the historic event prior to the Ordnance Survey of 1867. In 1773, the celebrated Dr Samuel Johnston and his friend James Boswell were at Slains Castle as guests of the Earl of Erroll. They were shown every place of interest on the coast but in Boswell's *Journal of a tour of the Hebrides* no mention is made of *St Catherine's Dub* or the wreck of the Spanish galleon—surely a subject on which the erudite Doctor would have made some pungent comment. In his valuable and detailed *Description of the East Coast of Scotland* (1782), Francis Douglas does not mention *St Catherine's Dub* as being a place of interest, while Peter Buchan has also nothing to say of it in his *Annals of Peterhead* (1819)—and few knew the Buchan coastline and its history more intimately. Similarly, in the *Statistical Account of Aberdeenshire,* published in 1843, there is no mention of *St Catherine's Dub.*

As already mentioned, a gun was found in the pool in 1840 and another in 1855. Consequently, when J. B. Pratt published his *Buchan* in 1858, he referred to the local fishermens' tale about the wreck of the Spanish vessel in *St Catherine's Dub.* The story was subsequently given in Alexander Smith's *History of Aberdeenshire* (1875), was repeated—with embellishments for tourist propaganda—in the *Great North of Scotland Railway Guide* (1881), and in James Dalgarno's *Brig o' Balgownie to the Bullers of Buchan* (1891) with illustration—'Spanish Armada Gun'. The story continued and is now accepted as an authentic part of the history of the Buchan coast.

However, in view of the foregoing facts, it is obvious that the Ordnance Survey's reference "Site of the wreck of the St Catherine, one of the Ships of the Spanish Armada A.D. 1588" is, to say the least, a statement of doubtful accuracy. It is possible, of course, that there may be some basis for the name *St Catherine's Dub.* Perhaps it was a corruption of an earlier name which, when linked with the finding of the Spanish coins, the salvaging of the guns and the anchors, snowballed into the romantic tale we know today? Might not the original name have been simply *'The Caterans' Dub'* (the robbers' pool)? After all, the Aberdeenshire fisher-folk enjoy a good story!

4

A Parish of Knights

*"The Knights' bones are dust,
And their good swords rust."*

At the Palace of Holyrood-house, Edinburgh, on 26th June, 1947, the Priory of Scotland of the Most Venerable Order of the Hospital of St John of Jerusalem was re-established. It had been in abeyance for nearly four hundred years.

The history of the Order of St John, the oldest Order of Chivalry in Christendom—it is two hundred years older than the Order of the Garter—is a long and interesting one. It goes back over 1,300 years—to the year 600 A.D., when Pope Gregory the Great established a small hospice in Jerusalem *'Pro utilitate hominum'* (for the welfare of mankind). From this humble beginning grew the most powerful Order of chivalry the world has ever known.

It may be said that the Order of the Hospital of St John of Jerusalem was the first-born of the First Crusade, the two kindred Orders, the Knights Templars and the Teutonic Knights being slightly later foundations.

It is generally accepted that the Knights Hospitallers and the Knights Templars were introduced to Scotland by David I (1124–1153). He had become acquainted with both Orders of chivalry during his sojourn in England.

The Earliest charter to the Hospitallers appears to have been granted in 1153 for this date is mentioned in a subsequent charter to the Preceptor of Torphichen. At all events, by the year 1160, both Orders of chivalry were firmly established in Scotland for in that year the signatures of 'Richard of the

Hospital' and 'Robert, Brother of the Temple' appear as witnesses to a royal charter to the Priory of St Andrews.

It is known, of course, that David I sent a Scottish contingent to the Second Crusade and the names of some of his Crusading knights are preserved, among them Anketillus de Menyeis (Menzies). Two of this distinguished Scotsman's descendants took part in the Fifth Crusade—Sir Robert and Sir David de Menzies, while Sir Alexander de Menzies, along with his fellow-countryman Sir William Gordon, 5th of Huntly, took part in the Eighth Crusade, the latter losing his life in the fierce fighting around Jerusalem. Whether these Crusaders were Hospitallers or Templars cannot now be determined but the preservation of their names is of very great interest particularly to Deeside with its associations with both these powerful Orders.

David I was succeeded by his grandson Malcolm IV (1153–1165) and during his reign and those of his two successors which covered a period of nearly a hundred years, the Hospitallers and Templars prospered. From the Crown, the Church and the great families, they obtained many valuable grants of land and revenues and it was through one of these gifts that both Orders established themselves on Deeside.

Sometime during the 12th century, the Scoto-Norman family of de Beyseth (Bisset) acquired the barony of Aboyne on Deeside. The family rose to prominence during the reign of Alexander II (1214–1249) but the influence they exercised brought them many enemies and caused their downfall. By the end of the 13th century they had all but faded from the Scottish scene.

The Beyseth family were generous patrons of the Church and one of them, Walter, Lord of Aboyne, appears to have had some association with the Knights Templars if, indeed, he was not actually a member of that Order. However, between 1221 and 1236, Walter de Beyseth founded a Preceptory of the

Knights Templars at Maryculter in Kincardineshire and this was followed, in 1240, by Radolphus, Bishop of Aberdeen, granting the Knights Templars the church of Formaston near Aboyne. Some years later, the Templars also received the church of Tullich near Ballater.

Eventually, as the Knights Templars grew in fame and power they, in turn, became the envy of their enemies and soon jealousy—that motive force in so many crimes—sought their elimination. In 1312, Pope Clement V, in collaboration with Philip IV of France, decided that the Templars must be suppressed and issued a Bull abolishing the Order. With this, the Knights Templars ceased to exist—struck down by the very power they had fought to preserve.

The Trial of the Templars in the various European countries is a matter of history and it is to Scotland's lasting credit that here, the Templars' property was merged with that of the Hospitallers. In most European countries, the sequestration of the Templars' lands was regarded as an opportunity to acquire new lands and the powerful did so unhesitatingly. It was thus, as the successors to the Knights Templars, that the Knights of the Hospital of St John of Jerusalem came to Deeside in 1312.

The Preceptory of Maryculter on Deeside consisted of approximately 8,500 acres of land on the south bank of the River Dee about six miles west from Aberdeen. This valuable possession included such well-known Deeside estates as Shannaburn, Heathcot, Auchlunies, Blairs, Kingcausie, Maryculter, Altries and Wedderhill.

In 1287, the Knights Templars had petitioned the Abbot of Kelso, as feudal superior of the Lands of Culter, to allow them to erect a chapel on the Preceptory lands. The Templars claimed that their tenants were denied the full rights of the Church by the frequent flooding of the River Dee, and as there was no bridge, they were often prevented from attending the chapel of St Peter on the opposite bank. The Templars' petition was granted and the chapel built. It was, of course, dedicated to the Templars' patron—the Blessed Virgin Mary—hence the two names in the locality Maryculter and Peterculter, which eventually became separate parishes.

When the Knights Hospitallers took seisin of the Templars' property at Maryculter, the chapel had just been built. It was a simple, rectangular structure which, even in its present fragmentary state, retains something of its former dignity. It is obvious, from the carved fragments lying around, that it was a Gothic building of some architectural importance, similar in many respects, to its near and more fortunate neighbour in the same county—Cowie Kirk, north of Stonehaven.

By the middle of the 14th century, the Knights Hospitallers were firmly established on Deeside. At their Maryculter Preceptory they proved to be excellent landlords for they had the means and skill to develop their lands. And their tenants regarded themselves as particularly fortunate for, with the Order in possession, there was little chance of their holdings being confiscated or their labours squandered by spendthrift lairds. The Hospitallers, of course, expected their tenants to play their part and were, when occasion arose, particularly strict regarding tillage and rotation of crops. It was the bounden duty of every tenant to erect on his highest building the eight-pointed cross of the Order—an ever-present reminder of his obligations to the Hospitallers. Some of these crosses survived until comparatively recent times.

Fortunately for posterity, the exact boundaries of the Preceptory—the 'landis pertanand to the Hospital of Saynt John'—are preserved and are so clearly defined that the marches of the property can be followed today without difficulty. This careful delineation was the work of John Fleming, knight, Master of the Maryculter Preceptory circa 1415, who would seem to have had a flair for settling disputes regarding boundaries for his signature as arbiter appears on several local documents.

PLATE 1

(a) Abergeldie Castle, near Ballater, Aberdeenshire.

(b) 'The Pit', Abergeldie Castle, below the spiral staircase in the round tower.

PLATE 2

(a) Drumnahoy, Cluny, Aberdeenshire.

(b) Andrew Robertson (self portrait) in Highland dress.

For two hundred years, the Hospitallers maintained their property at Maryculter, then in 1528 came the first signs of change when the Scottish Parliament of James V (1513–1542) passed an Act empowering Religious Orders to feu out their lands to men of substance who could improve them. In 1535, therefore, the Hospitallers of Maryculter availed themselves of this new Act to feu the part of their property called Blairs to Gilbert Menzies of Findon in the same county. That Gilbert Menzies should have been selected as the Hospitallers' feuar is of special interest for he was the descendant of the already-mentioned Anketillus de Menyeis who served with the Scottish army along with the Hospitallers during the Second Crusade.

Gilbert Menzies was Provost of Aberdeen for six terms covering a period of twenty-four years. He married Marjory Chalmers and died in 1543, his wife surviving him by ten years. Both Gilbert Menzies and his wife were interred in the Preceptory Chapel of St Mary, Maryculter, where in the Menzies Aisle, their life-size effigies lay until their removal at the end of last century to the West Church of St Nicholas, Aberdeen, where they remain. It is interesting to note that Gilbert's effigy, which portrays him in full armour of the period, shows him wearing an eight-pointed cross, doubtless an indication of his associations with the Order of St John.

The Reformation was now imminent and by the year 1548 the closing of the Preceptory seemed likely. At that date there were only six Knights and a Chaplain in residence. Eventually, Sir James Sandilands, the last Prior of the Order in Scotland, resigned all the Hospital's property to the Crown and in 1563 Mary Queen of Scots (1542–1567) erected them into a temporal barony in his favour.

In 1618, the old Preceptory at Maryculter was purchased by Thomas Menzies of Pitfodels, grandson of the already-mentioned Gilbert Menzies of Findon and Blairs, and when the last Menzies laird disposed of it in 1811, the final link with the past was severed—except that Maryculter was then acquired by General the Hon William Gordon, a descendant of Sir William Gordon who, as mentioned before, fell in the fighting at Jerusalem in the Eighth Crusade.

With the Reformation, the Knights of St John vanished from the scene of their labours and four hundred years were to pass before they reappeared on Deeside.

It is a curious fact that, despite bitter religious controversies and changes, works of charity and humanity survive and so, in 1831, a Grand Priory of the Hospital of St John of Jerusalem was re-established in Great Britain. In 1888, Queen Victoria granted a charter regularising its establishment in her Realm— as a Christian and undenominational Order and became its first Sovereign Head. This dignity is now held by her great-great-grand-daughter, Her Majesty The Queen.

> *"The old order changeth, yielding place to new,*
> *And God fulfils Himself in many ways,*
> *Lest one good custom should corrupt the world."*

Perhaps it is significant that the eight-pointed cross of the Hospitallers—once so familiar on Deeside—should re-appear in the area symbolising the continuance of charitable works for mankind.

5

Highland Games

"Land of brown heath and shaggy wood,
Land of the mountain and the flood."—Sir Walter Scott.

With unfailing regularity, the Scottish Season comes round year after year when the Court moves from the south to Balmoral Castle in Aberdeenshire. It has done so since the days of Queen Victoria. Subsequently becoming more Scottish than the Scots, the great Queen developed an unbounded enthusiasm for all things Scottish. Consequently the whole country—"that knuckle-end of England, that land of Calvin, oat-cakes and sulphur"—benefitted from the royal attention.

Of course, Queen Victoria was extremely proud of her Scottish connections and her descent from the Royal House of Stuart. She liked to be regarded as *Ard-ban-righ Albainn*— High Chief of Scotland—which indeed she was, for the last of the Stuarts, Henry, Cardinal of York, had settled the succession by the Law of Tanistry on George III in 1807. Perhaps it was for this reason Victoria disliked when the names "Old" and "New Pretender" were mentioned in her presence—to the Queen they were Prince James and Prince Charles!

At all events, it is recorded that in 1849 Queen Victoria attended her first Highland Gathering. She was immediately fascinated by the romance and glamour of the occasion and with such royal approval and subsequent patronage, Gatherings began to flourish all over Scotland as never before.

Tradition asserts the Highland Gatherings were instituted by Malcolm III—'the Canmore' (1057–1093)—as a means of attracting the finest and fittest men into his service. However, evidence suggests that they were held long before King Malcolm's reign and derive from two sources—the ever-present desire of the Celt to excel in the arts of war and his natural keenness for physical fitness. These, together with the in-born passion for pageantry, music, dancing and colour are the fundamental ingredients of the Highland Gathering.

From time immemorial, until after the Jacobite Rising of 1745 when Gatherings were prohibited by Act of Parliament, every Clan had its annual get-together. Indeed when not engaged in actual warfare it would appear that the Highlanders did little else but hold Gatherings! Raphael Holinshead, the 16th-century English chronicler, describes the situation thus: "whensoever the Clans entered into league and amatie with their enemies, they would not live in such security that thereby they would suffer their bodies and forces to degenerate, but they did keep themselves in their former activity and nimble-ness of lives, either with continual hunting or with running from the hills unto the valleys, or from the valleys unto the hills, or with wrestling and such kind of pastimes, whereby they are never idle."

In character, the early Gatherings were partly military, partly athletic and partly recreative. The Celtic desire to excel in the arts of war is no longer apparent in the present-day Gatherings for that accomplishment is the prerogative of a highly specialised Government Department—the Ministry of Defence. In bygone times, however, ability to handle and use the various weapons of war, was an important part of the Gathering. There were archery contests, cudgel-play—at which every youth excelled—spear-throwing, broad-sword, two-handed sword and dirk competitions while strict attention was paid to smartness of turn-out, an essential where Highland dress is concerned. It is curious that only the last mentioned should have survived in the form of the event prosaically styled 'The Best Dressed Highlander'.

Closely allied to the military aspect of the Gathering is the piping. In Celtic Scotland the piper held an important place. Every Chief had his piper, frequently a hereditary office such as was held by the MacCrimmons, hereditary pipers to the McLeod of McLeod, and the McArthurs, hereditary pipers to McDonald of the Isles. Usually the office carried with it a substantial grant of land within the Clan territory. Several of the instruments played by the hereditary pipers were credited with supernatural powers such as the celebrated *feadhan dubh*—the Black Chanter of Clan Chattan, the possession of which was guaranteed to bring prosperity to its owner and his family. As early as 1362, mention is made of the King's Pipers who received 40 shillings annually for their services, while in the reign of James VI we learn that two pipers preceded the king when he went to church. Much has been written about the Scottish Bagpipe—some of it highly interesting and complimentary, while some of it—usually expressed by the Sassenach—is definitely the reverse. However, it is pleasant to read that at least one Englishman, the celebrated Dr Samuel Johnson, "delighted to stand for some time with his ear close to the drone of a Great Highland Bagpipe in order to enjoy the exquisite torture".

Another hereditary officer in the Clan was the banner-man, who carried the Chief's banner on which was displayed his armorial bearings. The well-known family of Bannerman were the hereditary banner-men to the early Kings of Scotland, an office which they held until the reign of Malcolm III when it was conferred on the Scrymgeour family. The banner-men were much in evidence at the early Gatherings where they had the honour of raising their Chief's banner as he entered the arena to the strains of the *cuairt piobaireachd*. Happily, this ancient custom has recently been revived for it adds greatly to the interest and pageantry of a Gathering.

Perhaps the most picturesque part of the Highland

Gathering is the dancing. It would appear that in Celtic Scotland certain dances were regarded as having a religious significance and were performed in the churchyard. Subsequently these developed into dances of honour to be performed only on important occasions, thus we find King James II (1437–1460) being greeted with the dance called *rincefada*—a ceremonial dance played on the *cuisley ciuil*, a simple form of bagpipe.

Maria Taglioni, the celebrated *danseuse,* described good dancing as *"the absence of all appearance of effort"* and this must surely apply to Highland Dancing which is the embodiment of lightness and grace.

The oldest dance to be seen at a Gathering today is possibly the *Ghillie Calum*, the familiar Sword Dance. Of martial origin, it is said to have been a dance of victory, the victor's sword being placed over that of the vanquished. Closely associated with the *Ghillie Calum* was the Dirk Dance which has long since disappeared from Gathering programmes. This forgotten dance, vigorous in execution, was in the nature of an 'action' dance indicative of an encounter with the enemy, and was danced to a tune called *Padruig MacCombish.* Another forgotten dance is the *Rungmor*, in which the dancer touched the ground with his thighs without losing his balance. The *Rungmor* called for great dexterity on the part of the dancer and from contemporary descriptions of the dance it would appear to have been reminiscent of some of the Russian folkdances.

One of the most popular dances is the *Righil a' Thulaichen*, or *Hulachen* as it is sometimes called from the Gaelic pronunciation. It is actually the Reel o' Tullich which is said to have originated at the hamlet of Tullich, near Ballater on Deeside, but at least two other places claim the distinction of being the scene of the first *Hulachen*—Tulloch, near Dingwall, and Tulloch, near Abernethy in Strathspey. According to tradition, this famous Reel originated as an impromptu act by the congregation of Tullich Kirk who, tired of waiting for the minister to put in an appearance on a particularly cold and stormy morning, started to dance in the kirkyard in an endeavour to promote circulation. The congregation was soundly rebuked for this terrible act of sacrilege and not a single person who took part survived the year!—or so we are told. It is possible that the *Hulachen* may have had its origin in one of the early religious dances already referred to.

The *Seann Truibhas* is a particular favourite despite its meaning—'Old Trousers'. *Seann Truibhas* is said to have originated after the Jacobite Rising of 1745 when the wearing of the kilt was prohibited and trousers became compulsory. However, there is evidence that *Seann Truibhas* is much older than the 18th century, the appropriate costume for this most graceful dance being the tight-fitting tartan *truibhas* frequently worn in the Highlands at a much earlier date. Robert Tannahill, the Paisley poet, refers to it thus:

> *"Sawney McNab wi' his tartan trews,*
> *Has hecht to come down in the midst o'*
> *the caper,*
> *An' gi'e us three wallops o' merry Shan Trews,*
> *Wi' the true Highland fling o'*
> *Macrimmon the piper."*

The Highland Fling is believed to have originated in Strathspey where so much lively music was composed. It was this dance and the Highland Reel which caused Francis Peacock, the Aberdeen Dancing Master of Peacock's Close, to write of some of his pupils from the Western Isles and the Highlands "that they excel in so superior a degree, that I myself have thought them worthy of imitation". Peacock was appointed Dancing Master of Aberdeen in 1747—two years after the '45 Rising.

But what of the athletic events which play so large a part of the Gatherings? Most of these have claimed the attention of Scotsmen from earliest times. Tossing the Caber, for example, was known in the 15th century—but as 'ye casting of ye bar'. Racing and Wrestling too, were practised in the remote past, and the *clach-neart*, the 'Stone of Strength' is still a favourite—now known as Putting the Stone. At the entrance gateway to every Chief or Chieftain's stronghold was a *clach-neart* and visitors were invited to try their strength as a token of friendship. A sport which has died out is *clach cuid fir*, which might be called the 'Manhood Stone', for when a youth could lift the 200 pound stone and place it on the top of another, about 4 feet from the ground, he was reckoned to be a man and entitled to wear the bonnet. Long and broad jump are other athletic events which have always engaged the attention of the Highlanders, and *geal-ruith*—Hop, Step and Leap, appears to be of purely Celtic origin. Throwing the Hammer is said to have been the special sport of blacksmiths, some of whom became so enthusiastic as to forget the existence of the smiddy!

So, down the centuries, Gatherings were held all over the Highlands. Then came the Jacobite Risings bringing 'dool and destruction' to the country. The Disarming Act of 1746 struck at the very heart of the ancient Clan system for it decreed that "no man or boy" shall "wear or put on the clothes commonly called Highland clothes (that is to say) the Plaid, Philabeg, or little Kilt, Trowse, Shoulder-belts, or any part whatever of what peculiarly belongs to the Highland Garb; and that no tartan or party-coloured plaid or stuff shall be used". The penalty for 'offending' was transportation.

The obnoxious Act was repealed in 1782 but it was some time before the Gatherings were revived—Inverness appears to have been the first in 1788, Braemar in 1817, Lonach in 1841, Ballater in 1864, Aboyne in 1867 and Luss in 1875 to mention but a few.

Today, Highland Gatherings are, of course, first-class tourist attractions and social events, but like every other phase of Scottish life are rapidly undergoing change. The current trend is for new, exciting and extraneous items to be introduced to the programmes of events, yet at the moment sufficient survives at most Gatherings for them to be regarded as basically Celtic in origin—but for how long?

6

Inchdrewer Castle

"This castle hath a pleasant seat; the air
Nimbly and sweetly recommends itself
Unto our gentle senses."—Shakespeare.

High on a lush ridge of land between the River Deveron and the Burn of Boyndie, stands Inchdrewer Castle, one of the most fascinating strongholds in Banffshire, a county notably rich in castellated buildings. It lies about three miles south-west from Banff.

The name Inchdrewer is of ancient origin coming from the Gaelic *innis-druidhair*, the 'Druids' pasture', and from the numerous prehistoric remains surrounding the castle—stone circles, monoliths and burial cairns, and from the various 'finds' made over the years—it is obvious that the *innis-druidhair* was the centre of a very thriving community some 3,000 years ago.

Inchdrewer is situated in the parish of Banff, an area of around 6,073 acres, which was formed from two ancient Thanages—Mowbray and Boyne—first mentioned in the 13th century when the former belonged to Walter Barclay of Towie in Aberdeenshire, and the latter to Malcolm of Frendraught in the same county. The lands of Inchdrewer were part of the Thanage of Mowbray and would appear to have been held by the Barclays—who came to Scotland during the reign of William the Lion (1165–1214)—until 1414 when Inchdrewer was granted by them to Alexander Lindsay, Earl of Crawford. However, in 1421 Lindsay disposed of Inchdrewer to Sir Alexander Ogilvie of Auchterhouse whose only daughter and heiress Margaret, married James Stewart, Earl of

Buchan—second son of Sir James Stewart 'The Black Knight
of Lorne'. The Earl was therefore uncle to King James III
(1460–1488). In due course, Inchdrewer passed to the Earl of
Buchan but by 1474 the Innes family of that Ilk were in possession. However, about this time, and for some obscure
reason, Inchdrewer would seem to have been forfeited to the
Crown, yet in 1489 Alexander Innes of that Ilk granted to Sir
Walter Ogilvie, 1st of Boyne, three 'four parts' of Inchdrewer.
This grant, made in 1502, was subsequently confirmed by King
James III. In connection with the transaction, a curious agree-
ment was drawn up by Sir Walter in which he binds himself
and his heirs to Alexander Innes in consideration of the latter
having 'by plane chartir of gift' sold to Sir Walter three 'four
parts' of Inchdrewer in the Thanage of Mowbray. Alexander
agrees to pay Ogilvie 'ten score merks' on a day 'betwixt the
sonne Risying and Gangying to Rest' on the High Altar in the
parish church of Banff, when Sir Walter will 'overgive' the
lands of Inchdrewer. This curious document is signed by Sir
Walter who adds "I have appensit my sele to this present Writ
at Craig Boyne 3 July 1502".

Sir Walter Ogilvie, 1st of Boyne, the new owner of
Inchdrewer, was a man of unusual abilities. Born about the
year 1460, he was the second son of Sir Walter Ogilvie of
Auchleven in the Garioch district of Aberdeenshire, third son
of Sir Walter Ogilvie of Lintrathen in Forfarshire. At an early
age, Sir Walter was gifted the barony of Auchleven by his
father and in 1485 married Margaret, daughter and co-heiress
of Sir James Edmondston of Boyne and Tulliallan. He received
Boyne in right of his wife the same year.

Sir Walter had a distinguished career and filled many
important posts in the royal household. In 1486 he was
appointed Squire of the Body to King James III and following
the battle of Sauchieburn (1488), Ogilvie became the new
king's close personal friend and adviser. He held the same

appointment to James IV (1488–1513) and thereafter received many testimonies of royal favour including grants of land within the counties of Aberdeen and Banff. Sir Walter Ogilvie, 1st of Boyne and Inchdrewer died in 1508. By his marriage with Margaret Edmondston, Sir Walter had two sons—George Ogilvie of Durn—who succeeded his father as 2nd laird of Boyne—and who married Elspet, daughter of Alexander Irvine of Drum in Aberdeenshire; and Sir William Ogilvie of Strathern who married Alison Roule, one of Queen Margaret's ladies. Sir William succeeded to Inchdrewer.

Sir William Ogilvie of Strathern was an important man in Scotland. During the Regency of John, Duke of Albany, and the minority of King James V (1513–1542), he was High Treasurer of Scotland and undertook many important missions to England and France. However, the barony of Strathern in the Sheriffdom of Inverness, which had been granted to him in 1512, proved to be a source of much trouble and Sir William became involved in a bitter feud with his neighbours the Mackintoshes. Taking full advantage of the tragedy of Flodden (1513), the Mackintoshes invaded Strathern, plundering and burning Ogilvie's property and in 1517, at the height of these troubles, Sir William died. He was succeeded by his son John Ogilvie of Durn who in 1546 sold Inchdrewer to John Gordon of Huntly, son of George, 4th Earl of Huntly, the price being paid by Alexander Ogilvie of Findlater. However, later the same year, the Earl of Huntly granted a feu charter of Inchdrewer to James Currour, member of a family long associated with Banff, but unhappily Currour was killed at the battle of Pinkie the following year. However, thanks to the Decree given in the name of the young Mary Queen of Scots, two days before the battle, 'in favour of the heirs of those killed in conflicts against the English', James Currour's young son Walter succeeded to Inchdrewer.

In 1565 Walter Currour received a charter confirming his right to Inchdrewer. He appears to have become a somewhat quarrelsome character—especially with the Ogilvies—and in 1589 resigned Inchdrewer to his son George who in 1606 sold the property to Sir Walter Ogilvie of Findlater—later Lord Deskford. Inchdrewer again changed hands in 1622 when it was acquired by George Ogilvie, younger of Banff, in whose favour it was erected into the barony of Inchdrewer. With the advent of the barony in the year 1627, mention is first made of a 'manour-house'—the present castle of Inchdrewer.

For lack of evidence, it is difficult to say whether any stronghold existed at Inchdrewer before the present castle was built. It is possible, of course, that a motte—a structure of earthwork and timber—stood on the ridge where Inchdrewer now stands, but documentary proof is lacking and agricultural development has obliterated any evidence which may have existed. Certainly, the proximity of St Colm's Chapel, St Colm's Well, and the Gallow Hill—now mere sites—point to a feudal settlement, but as Inchdrewer was not erected into a barony until the year 1627, the existence of an earlier castle seems unlikely.

Inchdrewer appears to belong to at least two distinct periods of building. The kernel is a tower-house, reminiscent of a number of other castles in the north-east, among them the House of Schivas, Tolquhon Castle and Boyne Castle. This tower-house was probably built by Sir William Ogilvie of Strathern *circa* 1510 and it is interesting to note that the master-mason (architect) responsible for the work was the same person who built Schivas, Tolquhon and Boyne—Thomas Leper, originally Thomas-the-leper, whose work-period in the north-east covered from 1505 to around 1570. His mason's mark is found on Schivas, Tolquhon, Boyne and Inchdrewer.

Although re-planned and added to *circa* 1627, the tower-house of Inchdrewer in its original form was almost identical in plan and details with Schivas and Tolquhon. It consisted of an L-planned building—a main house and wing—with the entrance doorway in the re-entrant angle. A dog-legged stone staircase in the wing led from the ground floor to the hall on the floor above, the upper storeys being reached by a spiral stair set in the re-entrant angle. This dog-legged staircase was removed *circa* 1627 to enlarge the hall, a spiral stair taking its place in a new circular tower built on the south side of the tower-house. This tower, crowned by an open parapet, is a feature of Inchdrewer today.

In 1627, when Inchdrewer was erected into a barony, George Ogilvie appears to have begun an extensive building programme, but whether or not Thomas Leper was re-engaged as master-mason for the work is uncertain, although it seems likely that he was. Until his mason's mark is found on the later work, the question must remain in doubt. At this time, the rectangular courtyard with its flanking towers was added, enclosing two ranges of 'laigh-biggins', while a more impressive entrance doorway was introduced into the existing tower-house to link up with the new gate-house opposite. No doubt the castle pleasaunce was laid out at this time and records tell that several of its great trees were still standing towards the end of last century.

George Ogilvie, the originator of all these additions and alterations to Inchdrewer, was born about the year 1583. He was the son of Walter Ogilvie of Banff by his wife Helen, daughter of Walter Urquhart of Cromarty. George Ogilvie was twice married—first to Margaret, eldest daughter of Alexander Irvine of Drum, and second to Janet, daughter of Sir William Sutherland of Duffus, by whom he had an only son George born in 1624. In 1627 George Ogilvie—the elder—received a baronetcy from King Charles I (1625–1649).

In 1639—the year of the 'Troubles'—Sir George Ogilvie adopted the Royal cause. He took part in the local skirmish

known in history as the 'Trot of Turriff' and was present at the
battle of the Bridge of Dee against the Covenanters led by
Montrose. Following the battle, Sir George would appear to
have retired to Inchdrewer to await events but the advance of
General Munro and his army precipitated events and Ogilvie
took ship for England, subsequent reports recording he was
'liveing at Court with the King'.

In 1640 General Munro reached Inchdrewer Castle and
John Spalding, the Commissary Clerk of Aberdeen, tells the
story in his *Memorialls of the trubles in Scotland and in
England 1624-45.*—"The said 18th of August (1640), Major
Monro, with some few company, rides from Banff towards
Moray (leaving his Regiment behind him). . . . Many barons
and gentlemen met him, and honoured him by the way; he
hastily returned again to the camp, and by the way broke up
the iron gate of Inchdrewer, (a place where Banff used most
commonly to dwell in, and keep) and finally took it off, syne
sold it for five merks to a countryman whilk an hundred pound
had not put up. They break up doors and windows, entered the
house, and defaced all, and left nothing within it whilk they
might carry with them, without authority or law."

George Ogilvie's estates were sequestrated by order of
Parliament but his sovereign did not forget and in 1642 he was
raised to the Peerage as Lord Banff and granted the sum of
10,000 merks as compensation for his losses. Meantime, owing
to the damage done to Inchdrewer, Ogilvie's wife and family
had a hard time and were obliged to live in a small house at
Rettie near Banff, dependent on the generosity of relatives and
friends. However, in 1643, they were joined by George
Ogilvie—now Lord Banff—and six years later were able to
return to Inchdrewer where Lord Banff died in 1663.

Lord Banff was succeeded by his only son George who in
1648 married Agnes, daughter of Lord Falconer of
Halkerstoun. His early life was not without incident but later in

life he appears to have settled down at Inchdrewer where he died in 1668. He was succeeded by his son George.

George Ogilvie, 3rd Lord Banff, was born in 1649. He was still a minor when his father died and the barony of Inchdrewer—according to custom—was held by the Crown until he came of age. In 1669, at the age of twenty, Lord Banff married Lady Jean, youngest daughter of William Keith, 7th Earl Marischal, and took over the management of his barony. He appears to have been a strange, unstable character, a brutal man, given to the most violent outbursts of temper and assaults on his tenants. The disastrous fire at Inchdrewer in 1713 and his tragic death there was the culmination and aroused widespread interest throughout Scotland.

It would appear that, after attending his son's marriage in Edinburgh, Lord Banff decided to return home and late on Friday night the 13th January, 1713, arrived at Inchdrewer. He was alone and had been drinking heavily. Banff went to bed and shortly after midnight fire broke out on the upper floors of the castle. His Lordship was burned to death. However, rumours circulated that Banff had been murdered—stabbed and shot and the fire had been started deliberately to cover up the crime. The only other occupant of the castle that night was the housekeeper, Elizabeth Porter, who was eventually cited as the key witness in the Trial which followed in Edinburgh. Three young men in the district were suspected of the crime and subsequently arrested and brought to Trial—James Milne of Tipperty, William Brodie of Brydock Mill, and Robert Stewart. The verdict was 'not proven'—the key witness, Elizabeth Porter, had fled to Ireland, and the mystery of Lord Banff's death and the burning of Inchdrewer was never explained.

George Ogilvie, 4th Lord Banff, was born at Inchdrewer in 1670. Unlike his father, he lived quietly and did not marry until quite late in life. His wife was Helen, daughter of the celebrated Judge, Sir John Lauder Bt. of Fountainhall, by whom he had

PLATE 3

(a) St Catherine's Dub, near Coolieston, on the Buchan coast.

(b and c) The guns at Old Slains.

PLATE 4

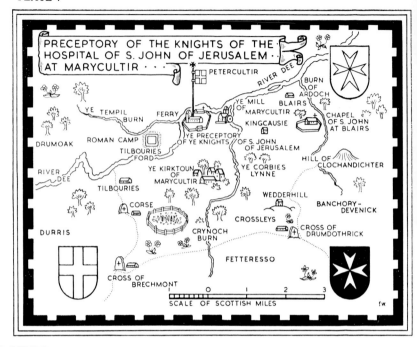

(a) Map of the Preceptory Lands at Maryculter, Kincardineshire.

(b) Window tympanum from the Preceptor's Lodging, Maryculter.

PLATE 5

The King's Piper by James Logan.

PLATE 6

Inchdrewer Castle, Banffshire, from Grose's *Antiquities* (1757).

two sons born at Inchdrewer in 1714 and 1715. A third son was born in 1717 and a posthumous son born in 1718. Lord Banff took no active part in the Jacobite Rising of 1715, but a visit to Inchdrewer from his Jacobite friend George Gordon of Buckie, produced some armament for the Prince's cause—"seven guns, ane paire of pistoles, four broad swords, and ane horse with furnitur". Lord Banff died in 1718 and was succeeded by his third son John, his two elder sons having died in infancy.

John, 5th Lord Banff, had a tragically short life for in 1741 he was drowned while bathing in the company of his friend Lord Deskford at Cullen. He was succeeded by his brother Alexander, the posthumous son of the 4th Lord Banff.

Alexander spent his early years at Inchdrewer but at the age of fifteen joined the Royal Navy. He had a brilliant but all too brief career and died at Lisbon in 1746. As Alexander was unmarried, the Banff title and Inchdrewer passed to his cousin Sir Alexander Ogilvie Bt. of Forglen—7th Lord Banff,—who was in turn succeeded by his second son William. William, 8th Lord Banff, died unmarried in 1803 when the Banff Peerage became extinct and Inchdrewer passed to his eldest sister Jean, wife of Sir George Abercrombie of Birkenbog.

It would appear that in 1746, following the death of Alexander Ogilvie, 6th Lord Banff, Inchdrewer Castle was rented to Dr. George Chapman who ran a boys' boarding school—a preparatory school—patronised by a number of the county families in the north-east. It would seem to have been a highly esteemed seminary and references to it are found in the correspondence of James, 2nd Earl of Fife, who sent his two nephews—Jamie (4th Earl of Fife) and Sandy (General Sir Alexander Duff)—to Inchdrewer for their early education.

How long Inchdrewer remained a boarding school is uncertain but it would seem that Dr. Chapman was followed by other tenants until 1873 when Inchdrewer is referred to as

7

Rob Roy Macgregor

'S rioghail mo dhream.
(Royal is my Race.)—motto of the Clan Macgregor.

The war-like figure of a Highlander perched precariously on a rocky gorge of the Leuchar Burn at Culter on Deeside seldom fails to attract the attention of visitors—particularly the young—for its colourful presence is unexpected if not quite startling. Its discovery is generally followed by a flood of questions—who is he?—why is he there?—what tartan is he wearing?—and so on, while the answer given is usually—it's Rob Roy, but don't ask me why he's here! Nevertheless, the story behind this figure of Rob Roy and why it should be located in an Aberdeenshire village far from his native Perthshire, is an interesting one.

The Clan Macgregor claims descent from Griogar, third son of King Alpin of Celtic Scotland and younger brother of Kenneth MacAlpine—hence their motto *'Royal is my Race'*. Originally the Macgregors were settled in Glenorchy, Argyllshire, and in the Clan's heyday their possessions were quite extensive. These territories were held allodially—by right of first occupation but without any charter—thus when their neighbours the Campbells rose to power and obtained Crown charters for lands long held by the Clan Gregor, it seems natural they should adopt strong measures to retain what they believed to be their ancestral possessions. Eventually the Campbells obtained authority from the Crown to evict the Macgregors. Consequently the Colquhouns, who held the King's Commission, came into conflict with the Clan and at the final confrontation in Glen Fruin in 1603—which ended in victory for the Macgregors—the Colquhouns lost two hundred men. The Government decided its only course was to exterminate the whole Macgregor Clan and steps were taken to bring this about. The terrible persecution of the Macgregors is a matter of history and need not be repeated, sufficient to say that from their territories in Perthshire, the Macgregors scattered to other districts including Deeside. Many found it advantageous to change their names—Gregor, Gregory, Greig, Grierson, Grigor, Gruer, King, Maconachie, Macpetrie, Pattullo, Peters, Skinner, Stalker, Walker and Whyte being the most usual on Deeside although close on a hundred have been recorded in other areas. Those who moved to Deeside soon became identified with the families in whose lands they settled and it is interesting to note that, despite the lapse of three hundred years, their descendants are still to be found in the valley.

However, early in the 17th century, three important families of the outlawed Clan Macgregor settled in north-east Scotland—the first was located in Aberdeen where they engaged in their former trade of saddlers and leather-workers; the second in the Howe of Cromar on Deeside as 'guests' of the Marquess of Huntly—an unfortunate arrangement as it proved which terminated in 1658 with the execution in Edinburgh of the freebooter Patrick Macgregor—the notorious 'Gilderoy', frequently confused with Rob Roy; and the third at Dalfad in Glengairn where they flourished under the protection of the Farquharsons of Invercauld.

But what of Rob Roy? Robert Roy (Gaelic: *ruadh*— 'red')—'Red Robert'—was the third son of Lt.-Colonel Donald Macgregor of Glengyle—the 'grey Macgregor'—and his wife Margaret, daughter of Archibald Campbell of Glenlyon and sister of Robert Campbell, 'the butcher', who commanded the Massacre of Glencoe (1692). He was born on 7th March,

1671, in the Stirlingshire parish of Buchanan. Rob's father was the younger brother of the Clan Chief of the Macgregors and in Rob's youth the family home was in the Perthshire parish of Balquhidder where they feued a farm from the Duke of Atholl. About the year 1693 and on account of the already mentioned prohibition of the Macgregors, Rob adopted his mother's family name and thus became Robert Campbell—but in Scottish legendary lore he remains Rob Roy Macgregor.

It is recorded that Rob received what education was deemed necessary for a young man of his station—not liberal, it is said, but adequate—particular attention being given to athletics and the use of arms, especially the broadsword, at which he showed unusual skill. His occupation is given as 'grazier' (cattle-breeder), but he appears to have branched out into a more lucrative 'racket'—that of protection—hiring himself to any who could afford his fee to protect their herds from cattle-rustlers. It would seem, however, that Rob himself was not averse to some cattle-lifting on the side and soon was in trouble with the law.

Fortunately the prospect of a Jacobite Rising would seem to have altered the course of Rob Roy's career for he threw in his lot with the Earl of Mar's party. Accordingly, towards the end of 1714, he received a commission to enlist the support of members of his scattered Clan in the north—in Aberdeen, Cromar and Glengairn—a task after his own heart.

In Aberdeen, the Macgregors prospered—particularly James, saddler and leather-worker, who on two occasions held office as Deacon-Convener of the burgh's Incorporated Trades. He had adopted the name of Gregory and was the founder of a very famous line—the Academic Gregorys.

During his visit, Rob Roy had to move about by stealth—and for three very good reasons—he was an outlawed Macgregor; he was a fugitive from justice on account of his cattle-lifting activities; and he was a secret agent for the

Jacobites. How indeed he got around unobserved remains a mystery, for his physical appearance was such that it would have been well nigh impossible for him to effect a disguise.

However, arriving in Aberdeen, Rob Roy first visited Professor James Gregory M.D. (1674–1733), great-grandson of James the saddler. The professor's father, James Gregory (1638–1675) had been professor of Mathematics at St Andrew's and Edinburgh, while his grandfather, John Gregory (1598–1650) had been parish minister of Dalmaik (Drumoak) on Deeside. Rob Roy was soon able to establish his kinship with Professor James Gregory and the story is told that while dining there Rob met the professor's young son James (1707–1755) with whom he was very much impressed, indeed Rob offered to take the lad to the hills 'and make him a fine gentleman'. The offer was tactfully declined. Young James eventually succeeded his father as Professor of Medicine at King's College, Old Aberdeen, while James's nephew—James Gregory M.D. (1753–1821) of Edinburgh, was none other than the creator of that once-familiar but abhorrent mixture—Gregory's Powder.

During his stay in Aberdeen, Rob Roy and the professor met frequently and it is said that one afternoon when they were walking together in Castle Street, the drums from the nearby barracks suddenly began a beat to arms and soldiers came running from all directions towards their headquarters. Rob, fearing he might have been recognised, bade his kinsman a hasty farewell, dashed down a nearby pend and disappeared.

Rob Roy then moved up Deeside to visit his kinsfolk at Dalmaik (Drumoak)—which furnishes the clue to the figure of the Highlander on the rocky gorge of the Leuchar Burn at Culter. In order to reach Dalmaik (Drumoak) from Aberdeen, Rob had to cross the Leuchar Burn—then in spate. However, to one of Rob Roy's athletic abilities, the flood waters were no impediment and he leapt across the swollen stream with ease—it is said near where the figure now stands. The story persisted down the years and when a local resident erected an old ship figure-head of a Highlander on the rocky bank, it was immediately linked with the story of Rob Roy's leap. When the figure-head perished—by which time it had become a feature of the locality and something of a 'tourist attraction'—an effigy of Rob Roy in full Highland dress was substituted. This in turn fell into decay and was replaced by the present figure.

From Dalmaik (Drumoak), Rob Roy continued his journey up the valley of the Dee visiting the scattered members of his Clan and when, in September, 1715, the Jacobite Standard was raised at Braemar, a substantial force of Macgregors were there in readiness to draw the sword for the Stuart cause.

Rob Roy's activities in the Jacobite Rising would appear to have been of a guerrilla nature but after the failure of the '15 Rob returned to his former 'business' of cattle-lifting for which he was eventually apprehended and taken to London. He was confined in Newgate Prison and having been found guilty of his various crimes was sentenced to transportation. He was put on board ship bound for Barbados but before it sailed Rob was pardoned and in due course returned to Balquhidder. There he lived quietly until his death on Saturday 28th December, 1734.

8

Aberdeen's Customs House

"He builded better than he knew;—
The conscious stone to beauty grew."—Emerson.

The old Customs House—No. 35 Regent Quay, Aberdeen—is one of those buildings which immediately holds the attention. In the late Renaissance style of architecture, it would be outstanding in any setting, but situated on one of the city's rather drab quay-sides, immediately poses the question—why should this fine Georgian mansion have been erected here? To answer the question one must go back a long way—to 1623 when Aberdeen's harbour was simply the tidal estuary of the Denburn.

By that time it had become evident that better harbour facilities must be provided if Aberdeen's commercial interests were to expand. Accordingly, a major harbour improvement scheme was envisaged and eventually carried out—the building of a great bulwark or 'Key' along the north side of the Denburn's estuary. Commencing at the Quay-head (opposite Shore Brae) and extending eastwards (to what is now the southern end of Commerce Street), it more or less followed the line of the present quay wall. The building of this 'Key' had the two-fold effect of deepening the water in the tidal estuary and reclaiming an extensive area of ground—bounded on the north by an ancient pathway subsequently called Virginia Street—which at high tide had hitherto been covered by water. Thus, by the year 1700, this reclaimed area known as the Shore Lands, had become a favourite resort for the citizens—their 'Carpet Walk', so called on account of its soft grassy surface.

*   *   *   *   *

The story now moves to Park in the parish of Ordiquhill in Banffshire. This property belonged to a branch of the Gordons, descendants of John, second son of the famous 'Jock' Gordon of Scurdargue. The Gordons of Park were perfervid Jacobites, 'out' in both the Risings of 1715 and 1745.

James Gordon—the subject of this story—was the son of Sir James Gordon, 2nd Baronet of Park, by his second wife Margaret Elphinstone. James, who was born at Park in 1723, subsequently acquired the lands of Cobairdy in the Aberdeenshire parish of Forgue, some nine miles south from the paternal estate and thus became known as James Gordon of Cobairdy. He married Mary Forbes, daughter of James, 16th Lord Forbes, and of this lady history records she was 'a very sweet tempered woman, but not very handsome'. They had a family of three—James, born in 1742 and who predeceased his father, Ernest born in 1743 and who eventually succeeded to the family estates and to Park, and William born in 1744 'sometime a Lieutenant in the Russian navy'. Through James Gordon's marriage with Mary Forbes an unusual situation arose for, when her father married, as his second wife, James's sister Elizabeth, James thus became both son-in-law and brother-in-law to Lord Forbes.

It came as a shock to his many friends when James Gordon of Cobairdy joined in the Jacobite Rising of 1745 "for he had no manner of tincture that way, but being a rambling lad was determined mostly by comradeship and something to do". He was then twenty-two years of age.

In October, 1745, James Gordon of Cobairdy joined Prince Charles at Holyroodhouse in company with a number of Banffshire lairds. Records show that he 'acted in the character of an officer' but in what regiment is not disclosed. James was present at Culloden and after the battle made his way to Rothiemurchus and from thence to Banff where he remained in hiding until a favourable opportunity presented itself for his escape to France. In 1747 he was living at Cleves where Louis XV gave him command of a company in the French Army and a pension.

At home, moves were being made on his behalf by influential relatives and friends and in 1762 Gordon came to London. In January of the following year he and his wife were in Edinburgh and from there they moved north to Aberdeenshire where they stayed at Putachie—the old name for Castle Forbes—with Lord Forbes. Eventually they reached Cobairdy. In 1772—twenty-seven years after the ill-starred Rising—James Gordon's kinsman, the Earl of Fife, wrote to Lord Suffolk asking for a pardon but the request was unsuccessful and Cobairdy's name remained on the Government's list of rebels.

*   *   *   *   *

Back in Aberdeen and with the two Jacobite Risings over, prosperity returned and the Magistrates planned a new access road to the harbour. Subsequently called Marischal Street, as the project necessitated the demolition of the Earl Marischal's mansion-house in Castle Street, this new street was opened in 1768. The major problem in the plan was the spanning of the ancient pathway (Virginia Street) and this was overcome by the building of a single span bridge designed by William Law, architect. The southern end of Marischal Street thus bisected the reclaimed Shore Lands which, along with the ground lying on either side of Marischal Street, were subsequently feued by the Magistrates. In consequence, the whole area eventually became a desirable residential quarter and the dwelling houses erected there were, without exception, of unusual merit.

Accordingly, the Shore Lands were divided up into 'Lots' of around '2,243 square ells' and feued to various people of substance. On 19th June, 1766, the '5th Lot of the Shore Lands' was feued to a well-known local mason and builder Alexander Kennedy—father of William Kennedy, advocate, and author of *Annals of Aberdeen*. Some five years later, Kennedy disposed of the southern part of his feu to 'William Vitty, Tide Surveyor at the Port of Aberdeen, and Eleanor Sands his spouse', but in a matter of months the Vittys parted with their 'tenement of land' to James Gordon of Cobairdy. Here, the unpardoned Jacobite built for himself the handsome mansion—the building now known as the old Customs House.

On 24th August, 1772, Gordon took the precaution of insuring his house against fire, the policy describing it as being 'situate on the Quay of Aberdeen—stone, slated and leaded' but 'not yet finished'. According to custom, the Sun Fire Office sign was placed over the entrance doorway—a gilded sun in its splendour cast in lead and embossed with the policy number 315283 clearly visible after two centuries. The value of the property is given as £700—its present-day value around £120,000!

James Gordon and his wife Mary Forbes would seem to have moved into their new home in the spring of 1773 and on 8th April, presumably to preserve his southern amenity—then a magnificent panorama over the estuaries of the Denburn and the River Dee to the Grampian hills beyond—he acquired 'part of the Quay opposite to the parapet wall before his house'. Unhappily, Fate intervened, and Gordon did not live to enjoy his house, for he died there on 11th May, 1773.

In August of that year his son Ernest was served heir to Cobairdy and all the other family properties including the new house on the Quay-side at Aberdeen. He had Sasine dated 20th December, 1773. However, a month later—on 24th January, 1774—'in consideration of £1,100', Ernest Gordon of Cobairdy disposed of the house to 'Theophilus Ogilvie, Collector of Customs at Aberdeen, and his successors in Office' and it became Crown property—Aberdeen's Customs House.

Although internally, James Gordon's town house has, of necessity, been altered over the years, the exterior remains virtually the same as when it left the builder's hands two centuries ago. In design, it follows the usual style of the period—a simple block plan in which the hall and staircase occupy the centre, the rooms being compactly disposed on either side. The house comprises a basement, three floors and an attic. Originally, the kitchen and other domestic offices occupied the basement while on the first floor were the dining-room, parlour and study. An impressive, L-planned drawing-room with connecting sitting-room and boudoir occupied the second floor, while the family bedrooms were located on the floor above. The servants' sleeping quarters were in the attic. All floors were served in turn by an elegant geometrical stair-case in dressed granite with moulded treads.

Entirely built of local stone from Loanhead Quarries, the south front of the house—in fine, hand-dressed granite ashlar—is well-proportioned with carefully studied fen-estration. The main feature of this front is the pedimented entrance doorway reached by a short flight of granite steps with moulded treads. The south front of the building facing Regent Quay is indeed an outstanding piece of architectural design and it is regrettable that the identity of its architect has never been established.

One may assume that the builder of James Gordon's house was the man on the spot, Alexander Kennedy, mason, but as to its architect one can only hazard a guess. One thing is certain; it was not the work of any of the local men practising at the time—the design is too masterly. It seems probable that James Gordon commissioned some architect in the south to prepare plans for a town house soon after his marriage in 1742 and certainly before his involvement in the '45.

The remarkable affinity between the entrance doorway of the Regent Quay house and a number of others designed by the famous architect James Gibbs (1682–1754) suggests a link between him and Gordon. Gibbs was an Aberdonian—although there is no evidence to suggest that he returned to the city after a brief visit in 1709—and he had Jacobite sympathies. It is known that Gibbs frequently prepared plans of houses for clients although he did not actually supervise the building work or even see it when completed. Balvenie House (1700) in Banffshire, Seaton House (1725) and the West Church of St Nicholas (1741) both in Aberdeen, are examples. It is obvious that the Gordons of Park—and of course Cobairdy—were acquainted with Gibbs and his work for Sir William Gordon Bt, grandfather of James Gordon, was a subscriber to Gibbs' *A Book of Architecture* published in 1728. Who knows? It may well be that the credit for designing Cobairdy's Aberdeen house—the old Customs House on Regent Quay—belongs to James Gibbs.

9

Thomas the Rhymer

"Hear the voice of the Bard!
Who present, past and future sees."—William Blake.

Reading through the histories of various ancient, north-east families, it is remarkable how often the name Thomas the Rhymer appears, indeed it occurs so frequently one wonders if this fantastic, shadowy figure from Scotland's remote past is fact or fiction.

Reminiscent of the Arthurian wizard Merlin, Thomas the Rhymer's birth, life and death are shrouded in mystery. He is said to have been born about the year 1220 in the small town of Erceldoun—now called Earlston—in the parish of the same name in Berwickshire, and is first noted *circa* 1240, as witness to a deed pertaining to Melrose Abbey. His son, also called Thomas, is mentioned in a charter of 1294 when the 'Rhymer Lands' in Erceldoun were granted to the Trinity, or Red Friars, of the monastery of Fail in Ayrshire. Fail was founded in the year 1252 and it is on record that the Rhymer was a frequent visitor to this religious house.

Particulars regarding the Rhymer's background and early life are scant but what may be lacking in fact is generously supplied by fiction. When very young, it is said that Thomas—an unusually handsome and charming boy—was carried off by the Queen of Elfland who carefully instructed him in all her mystic lore. Eventually, she allowed him back to the world of Man so he might practise the skills she had taught him—but only for a time. He must return to Elfland whenever she called.

Thomas the Rhymer's reputation as a poet rests on his *Sir*

Tristrem, a metrical romance of the 13th century, but it is as a
seer that he lives in the annals of north-east Scotland where his
predictions were numerous and cover a very wide field. It is
astonishing to find so many of his prophesies surviving in these
parts—and often repeated after the lapse of over seven
hundred years. Of course, not every prediction accredited to
Thomas the Rhymer is the genuine article, for during the 14th,
15th and 16th centuries fabrications were circulated—usually
of the 'dool and destruction' variety.

Although tradition asserts that Thomas the Rhymer was
capable of making 'long-range' predictions from his Tower at
Erceldoun, it is evident he travelled considerable distances on
foot and by horse although it is hinted he moved about the
countryside by some mysterious means of locomotion known
only to the denizens of Elfland. At all events, according to
legend, the Rhymer was wont to 'appear suddenly' at his
various destinations, his arrival being heralded by 'great storms
of thunder and lightening'—like all top-rank wizards, he
obviously had a flair for dramatic entry.

According to the custom of his time, and particularly on account of his close ties with Melrose and Fail, the Rhymer
would most probably have lodged in one or other of the
religious houses in the area through which he was travelling.
Certainly in north-east Scotland this would appear to have
been the arrangement for the predictions accredited to him
may well be linked to the three religious houses in the
region—Monymusk (founded in 1165), Fyvie (founded in
1175) and Deer (founded in 1200).

As no record exists of Thomas the Rhymer's visit to north-
east Scotland, the year in which he undertook the journey to
these parts can only be a matter of conjecture. It would seem
he visited Aberdeen *circa* 1258, when he was about thirty-eight
years old, and probably lodged with the Trinity, or Red Friars,
at their monastery in the Green (founded in 1181). Of course,

at this date, the Rhymer had not yet made his name as a seer, although it appears he already enjoyed a well-merited reputation as poet and bard. It was not until 1286 when he predicted the sudden and tragic death of Alexander III (1249–1286) that the Rhymer 'made the headlines' as a prophet—and subsequently became 'True Thomas'.

From the Trinity Friars' monastery at Aberdeen, it is probable the Rhymer made his way northwards along the south bank of the River Don to Monymusk. Here, he would seem to have made his first prediction in the district which refers to Monymusk itself and is expressed with the Rhymer's customary ambiguity—

> "*Monymuss sall be a buss*
> *To draw the dun deer doon*"

Although the Priory of Monymusk (Gaelic: *moine musgach*—'muddy peat-moss') had been founded nearly a century before the Rhymer's time, the countryside around it was still desolate and certainly no 'buss' to attract the 'dun deer'—the deer from the hill-fort on Bennachie. Of course, Thomas the Rhymer was never one to look for quick results so it was not until around 1756 that his prediction was said to have been fulfilled, when Sir Archibald Grant, 2nd Baronet of Monymusk, began the extensive afforestation of his estate which in truth transformed the desolate countryside. As one would expect, the spectacular outline of Bennachie also attracted the Rhymer's attention but the meaning of his prophesy remains obscure—

> "*A mither's ae son, wi' ae e'e,*
> *Sall find the keys o' Bennachie,*
> *Aneath a rash buss,*
> *I' the backward o' Tollus*"

'Tullos', now Tulloch, lies just south from Bennachie and east

PLATE 7

Rob Roy statue at Peterculter, Aberdeenshire.

PLATE 8

(a) Customs House, Regent Quay, Aberdeen.

(b) Front entrance doorway.

(c) Sun Fire Office sign in the pediment of the entrance doorway.

PLATE 9

Brig o' Balgownie, Aberdeen, showing the *poll gonaidh* (pool of bewitchment) below the bridge, and the approach to the old ford.

PLATE 10

(a) Kingswells House, Aberdeen.

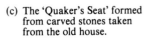

(b) Text stone from old
Meeting House.

(c) The 'Quaker's Seat' formed
from carved stones taken
from the old house.

of Keig village, but the 'keys', whatever they may be, remain in the 'backward'. A 'mither's ae son' would seem to be an individual of some significance to the Rhymer as he figures in several of his predictions.

The Old Rayne prophesy would also appear to belong to the Monymusk group—

> *"Fite kirk o' Rayne,*
> *Straught is your wa';*
> *But on bonnie Pasch Sunday*
> *Doon ye sall fa' "*

That a church actually existed at Old Rayne when the Rhymer visited the district is certain—'the kirk of St Andrew of Rane and Rothmas' referred to in a charter dated 1175. However, this church was demolished and in 1574 another erected on its foundations. This too was demolished and in 1788 a third church built on the same site—a white, harled building, the first of its kind in the neighbourhood—hence the 'Fite Kirk o' Rayne'. As this building did not appear until five centuries after the Rhymer's time, the authenticity of the prediction is extremely doubtful and may well be a 'fret' directed against the new church with its 18th century 'straught' walls as opposed to the traditional battered walls of the preceeding centuries.

The last prophesy in the Monymusk group relates to Inverurie—

> *"When Dee and Don sall rin in one,*
> *An' Tweed sall rin in Tay;*
> *The waters o' the Urie*
> *Sall bear the Bass away"*

At the date of the Rhymer's visit, the Bass of Inverurie was the principal stronghold of the Leslie family, Constables of the Lordship of the Garioch. The Constables have long since disappeared but the Bass remains, a prominent feature of the

Inverurie scene. From this it may be assumed that it was one of the Rhymer's 'delayed action' prophesies.

From Monymusk, the Rhymer would appear to have moved northwards to the Priory of Fyvie of which nothing now remains. A modern cross marks the site.

Much has been written about Thomas the Rhymer's visit to Fyvie Castle where, according to local legend, the entrance gate had stood 'wall-wide' for 'seven years and a day' awaiting his arrival. With his usual flair for dramatic effect, the Rhymer 'appeared suddenly' at the height of a violent storm which stripped the leaves from the trees, yet 'not a hair of the prophet's beard was seen to stir'. He slammed the great gate behind him with a resounding crash—and the storm immediately abated. The stage was now set and Thomas the Rhymer spoke his fateful lines—

> *"Fyvyne riggs an' Fyvyne tours,*
> *Hapless sall thy mesdames be,*
> *Fan ye sall hae within your methes,*
> *Frae harryit kirk-landis, stanis thrie—*
> *Ane in ye heiches' tour;*
> *Ane in ye Ladye's bower;*
> *Ane aneath ye wattir-yett,*
> *An' this stane ye sall never get."*

The meaning of this 'fret' has long been debated for it is worded with the Rhymer's usual ambiguity. Of course it has been variously and ingeniously interpreted, but despite the passing of seven centuries, the 'Curse of Fyvie' remains a mystery.

The Priory of Fyvie, where Thomas the Rhymer is presumed to have stayed, was founded in 1175 by King William the Lion (1165–1214). It stood on the left bank of the River Ythan about a mile due south from Fyvie Castle. At the date of the Rhymer's visit, *circa* 1258, the castle was a royal domain, the capital messuage of the Thanage of Fermartyn— not the present Fyvie Castle, of course, but its predecessor— a stronghold of the 'enclosure' type.

It would appear the 'Curse of Fyvie' was another of the Rhymer's 'delayed action' predictions for the terms of its directive would not seem to have been fulfilled until some three centuries after his time—when the priory's 'kirk-landis' were 'harriet' subsequent to the Reformation (1560). It is on record that the priory was then pillaged for building stone, while tradition asserts the 'stanis thrie' were carried off to their various destinations within the 'methes' of Fyvie Castle. Like the meaning of the 'fret', the 'stanis thrie' and their ultimate location have been diversely explained. One of the alleged 'stanis'—a 'weeping stone'—now reposes in the Meldrum Tower at Fyvie Castle. In bygone times it was regarded with considerable awe, but the stone is simply a porous block which absorbs and exudes moisture by a natural process according to atmospheric conditions. Whether it actually came from the ancient priory and whether its companion 'stanis' are, or were, of similar geological composition, we shall never know.

The 'hapless' fate forecast for Fyvie's 'mesdames' would seem to be the kernel of the 'Curse' and has been widely interpreted. The traditional belief is that no heir to Fyvie will ever be born within the castle nor will the estate ever pass in direct line from father to eldest son—so long as the 'stanis thrie' remain within the 'methes' of Fyvie. Although the histories of the great families who have owned the lands of Fyvie are cited as 'proof' of the effectiveness of the curse, it is open to question if their vicissitudes were very much different from any other county family.

The second prediction of the Fyvie group applies to Towie-Barclay Castle which lies some four miles north-west from Fyvie—

"Tolly Barclay o' the glen,
Happy to maids, but never to men."

It would seem the Rhymer was anxious to placate the 'maids' of Towie-Barclay having 'fretted' their luckless neighbours the 'Mesdames' of Fyvie. Of course the present castle of Towie-Barclay dates from around 1593, but it is possible an earlier stronghold stood on or near the same site in the Rhymer's time.

Gight Castle, now a picturesque ruin on the left bank of the River Ythan about three miles below Fyvie, appears to have been the next place to attract the attention of Thomas the Rhymer during his sojourn in these parts. Here he is credited with having made three prophecies relating to the Gordons of Gight, but as this family's associations with the district did not begin until long after the Rhymer's time, the authenticity of the predictions is extremely doubtful—unless, of course, 'frets' were made by the Rhymer against the Gordons at some previous date and subsequently were translated to Gight. This is a possibility for there is an interesting link between the Rhymer and the Gordon family.

Of French extraction, the Gordons settled in Scotland early in the 12th century—in Berwickshire, their barony eventually giving its name to the parish of Gordon. Adjacent to the parish of Gordon and in the same county, is the parish of Earlston—the Rhymer's birth-place—and he must have been well acquainted with his neighbours the Gordons. Thomas the Rhymer died about the year 1297, before the Gordons acquired their first hold in Aberdeenshire—the Lordship of Strathbogie. The Rhymer's personal knowledge of the family was therefore restricted to their Berwickshire period, but whether his predictions were made then and subsequently translated to Aberdeenshire remains obscure.

The first of the Gight prophesies takes the form of an unanswered query framed with quaint obliquity—

"Twa men sat doon of Ythan Brae,
T'ane did to t'ither say,
An' fat sic men ha'e the Gordons been?

The castle of Gight was built about the year 1540 by George Gordon, the second laird, who succeeded his father in 1513. The significance of the prediction—which has the appearance of being part of an unfinished poem—has never been explained.

The next two prophesies against Gight and attributed to Thomas the Rhymer might be called 'completed' forecasts for, according to local belief, their details are said to have been fulfilled. The first is—

"When the herons leave the trees,
The laird o' Gight sall landless be".

The last laird of Gight was Catherine, daughter and heiress of George Gordon of Gight, who in 1785 married Captain the Hon John Byron. They were the parents of the poet George, 6th Lord Byron. In 1787, due to the financial embarrassment of her husband, Catherine Byron was obliged to dispose of Gight, the property being acquired by her kinsman and near neighbour George Gordon, 3rd Earl of Aberdeen.

For centuries a colony of herons had inhabited the trees around Gight Castle but one morning, shortly after Catherine Gordon's marriage with John Byron, the colony suddenly migrated to the woods of Kelly on the Haddo House estates. Soothsayers of the day, noting the birds' removal and recalling the Rhymer's 'fret', opined that the 'riggs o' Gight' would soon follow the herons—and so indeed they did in 1787.

Gight Castle thus became the home of the Earl's eldest son, George, Lord Haddo, and his wife Charlotte Baird, daughter of William Baird of Newbyth, cadet of Auchmedden. This brings us to the third and most tragic of the Gight prophesies—

> *"At Gight three men a violent death sall dee,*
> *An' efter that the land sall lie in lea."*

Lord Haddo was himself the first victim of the curse for in 1791, while riding home, his horse suddenly shied 'on the Green of Gight', throwing its rider and killing him. Some years later, a man-servant at the castle met a similar fate while riding, and soon after at Mains of Gight, a workman was crushed to death when demolishing a boundary wall so that the land might 'lie in lea'—oddly enough having but shortly before repeated the curse to his companions.

It would appear the last prophesy made by Thomas the Rhymer during his sojourn at the Priory of Fyvie referred to the Baird family of Auchmedden. Situated in the maritime parish of New Aberdour, near Pennan Head in Aberdeenshire, Auchmedden was acquired by the Bairds in 1568. The prediction has it—

> *"While there's an eagle in Pennan,*
> *There'll be Bairds in Auchmedden"*

According to local tradition, a pair of sea-eagles nested on the rugged cliffs of Pennan Head for a great many years, their 'tenancy' coinciding with the Baird's ownership of Auchmedden. The story goes that, on the Bairds disposing of the property to George Gordon, 3rd Earl of Aberdeen, the eagles left their eyrie. However, when the Earl's son Lord Haddo, married Charlotte Baird of New Byth, the sea-eagles returned—but left again when Auchmedden passed to the Hon William Gordon.

From Fyvie, Thomas the Rhymer appears to have moved to the Abbey of Deer in the Buchan district of Aberdeenshire where he made a number of prophesies mostly of a calamitous nature. It would seem that Alexander Comyn, 2nd Earl of Buchan—close friend of Alexander III and son of the Abbey's founder—was not impressed by the Rhymer or by his predictions, frequently referring to him as 'Tammas-the-Lyar'. This, of course, was enough to raise the ire of any self-respecting wizard and the Rhymer was no exception to the rule. He let himself go in a special 'fret' against Earl Alexander and indeed against all the Comyns—

> *"Though Tammas the Lyar thou call'st me,*
> *A sooth tale I sall tell to the:*
> *By Aiky-side thy horse sall ride,*
> *He sall stumble an' thou sall fa';*
> *Thy neck-bane sall brak in twa,*
> *An' mangre all thy kin an' the,*
> *Thy ain belt thy bier sall be"*

Alexander, 2nd Earl of Buchan, died in 1289—yet it was at Aikey Brae on the western border of the parish of Old Deer that the final overthrow of the Comyns by Edward Bruce took place in 1307—the terrible 'hership o' Buchan'.

What Bennachie is to the Garioch district of Aberdeenshire, Mormond Hill is to Buchan. It lies due north from the Abbey of Deer and is an outstanding feature of the landscape—little wonder it received Thomas the Rhymer's attention even though his prediction is obscure—

> *"When Mormond Hill is clad in reed,*
> *Den Callie Burn sall rin wi' bleed;*
> *An' gin the saut rise 'been the meal—*
> *Believe the mair in Tammas' tale"*

The Frasers of Philorth, near Fraserburgh, were one of the few families to receive an encouraging pronouncement from the Rhymer with—

> *"Quhen there's ne'er a Cock o' the North,*
> *You'll find a Frizell (Fraser) in Philorth"*

It would seem the Rhymer moved round the north-east coast to St Fergus where, for lack of a more spectacular recipient, 'fretted' a granite boulder which, for some reason or another took his fancy. Standing on farm land belonging to the Keiths, Earl Marischals of Scotland, the boulder was for generations known as 'Tammas's Stane'—

> *"As lang's this stane stands on this craft,*
> *The name o' Keith sall be alaft;*
> *But fan this stane begins t' fa',*
> *The name o' Keith sall weer awa' "*

The removal of 'Tammas's Stane' for building purposes in the 18th century is said to have coincided with the death in 1778 of George Keith, 10th Earl Marischal—the last of his line. However, as if not content with his 'fret' against the Keiths, Thomas the Rhymer endorsed his prediction with another directed at the family's stronghold Inverugie Castle, near Peterhead—

> *"Inverugie by the sea,*
> *Lordless sall thy land be,*
> *And underneath thy hearth stane*
> *The tod (fox) sall bring her bairns hame"*

Of course Inverugie Castle was not in existence in the Rhymer's time nor was Fedderate Castle another of his Buchan targets—

> *"Fedderate will ne'er be ta'en,*
> *Till Fyvie wodes to the siege is gane"*

Built in the 16th century, Fedderate Castle was besieged and eventually blown up by Government forces in 1690—timber being brought from the woods of Fyvie for the operation.

One of the few cheering predictions accredited to the Rhymer during his sojourn in Buchan was directed at the little-known St Olaus's Well in the parish of Cruden—

> "St Olaus Well, low by the sea,
> Where pest nor plague sall never be."

But Thomas the Rhymer's benevolence appears to have been short-lived for on reaching Slains his habitual gloom returned as he made his pronouncement against the Hay family—Earls of Erroll and Hereditary High Constables of Scotland. On this occasion, the Rhymer focused his attention on an ancient oak tree growing near Slains Castle—

> "While the mistletoe bats on Erroll's aik,
> And that aik stands fast,
> The Hays sall flourish, and their good grey hawk
> Sall not flinch before the blast.
> But when the root of the aik decays,
> And the mistletoe dwines on its withered breast,
> The grass sall grow on Erroll's hearthstone,
> An' the corbie roup in the falcon's nest"

Both old and new Slains Castle are now ruinous but the 'fret's' interest rests on its heraldic significance—mistletoe is the badge of the Hays of Erroll while the falcon is their crest.

The Rhymer's next prediction was made at Foveran—at Turing's Tower, the ancient barony of the Turings of Foveran—

> "When Turing Tower falls to the land,
> Gladsmuir then is near at hand;
> When Turing Tower falls to the sea,
> Gladsmuir the next year sall be"

While the battle of Gladsmuir (Prestonpans), fought in 1745, was a decisive victory for the Jacobites, its connection with Turing's Tower remains a mystery.

Moving south after his tour of the north-east corner of Scotland, Thomas the Rhymer would seem to have reached the

River Don at Balgownie—*poll gonaidh* (pool of bewitchment). Here he made his well-known prophesy about the famous bridge—

> *"Brig o' Balgownie, wicht is thy wa',*
> *Wi' a wife's ae son an' a mare's ae foal*
> *Doun shalt thou fa' "*

As the Brig o' Balgownie was not completed until 1320 at the earliest—a quarter of a century after the Rhymer's death—it seems obvious if he actually crossed the Don at this point he must have done so by the ford below the sinister 'pool-of-bewitchment' which may have inspired the Rhymer's sense of impending doom. It is possible, of course, the Rhymer may have seen the foundations of the bridge begun about 1258 but his prediction remains, as yet, unfulfilled.

From the foregoing imaginary tour of Scotland's north-east corner by Thomas the Rhymer, it is obvious many of the 'frets' accredited to him were pronouncements made long after his time. From the 14th century onwards, the fabrication and circulation of 'frets'—in the name of Thomas the Rhymer—was accepted as being an effective way of striking fear into one's enemies—indeed the same basis as the witch's spell and wartime propaganda. However, there seems no reason to doubt the Rhymer did visit the north-east but which of the 'frets' accredited to him are genuine and which are later, fifth-column fabrications is anybody's guess.

Tradition tells that, unlike other mortals, Thomas the Rhymer did not die but was called back to Elfland to 'dree his weird'. Perhaps the best assessment of this strange, elusive character is given in *The Buik of Croniclis of Scotland* which succinctly assesses his unique position in the country's annals—'a man of great wonder to the people, and showed sundry things ere they befel—howbeit his prognostications were aye under obscure words'.

10

A Quaker Provost

*"Truly the vision tarrieth, but times and
seasons are in the Lord's own keeping."*

*"Tuesday, the 8th of October, 1657, At His Highness's Council
in Scotland. Ordered that George Fox do appear before the
Council on Tuesday, the 15th October next, in the Forenoon.
E. Downing, Clerk of the Council."*

From contemporary records we learn that 'He appeared
accordingly, and after Examination, they told him, that he
must depart the Nation of Scotland by that day Sevenight.
Nevertheless he continued travelling up and down through
several Parts of that Country, preaching among the People
wheresoever he came, and afterwards returned to Edinburgh,
where he was told that the Council had issued Warrants to
apprehend him for Breach of their Order, in not departing the
Country within the limited Time. To which his Answer was,
What do ye tell me of their Warrants? If there were a Cart-
load of them, I do not heed them. For he, knowing his Commission to be from God, was carried above the Fear of Man in
discharging it; and a peculiar hand of Providence was sometimes visible in the Manner of his Deliverance.'

It was thus that the tenets of the Society of Friends
(Quakers) became known in Scotland.

There is no record as to the scope of George Fox's mission
into Scotland, but it is generally accepted that he did not pene-
trate much further north than Edinburgh. It was, therefore,
some years after the above incident—in the year 1662—that

the Quakers became known in the north-east part of the country. In this year William Dewsbury proclaimed that it was 'the acceptable year of the Lord' and the Aberdeen Meeting came into being. 1662 appears to have been a year of great activity for the Quakers of north-east Scotland for several other Meetings were established besides that of Aberdeen— Aquhorthies, Dyce, Kingswells, Old Meldrum, Ury and Kinmuck which subsequently became the largest Meeting in Scotland and the most northerly in Europe.

In every new movement, whether sacred or secular, much of its success depends on the faith and ardour of the initial members, and the early adherents to the Quaker faith in Aberdeenshire were no exception. The new religion flourished. Prior to the establishing of the Aberdeen Meeting, the remarkable work of convincement had, of course, been privately going on among individuals, consequently, when the actual formation took place, religious fervour was at its greatest resolve. One of these early Quakers was Alexander Jaffray of Kingswells.

The earliest mention of the Jaffray family in Aberdeen is in the burgh records where is states that one, Alexander Jaffray, was admitted a burgess of the Baxter (baker) Trade in the year 1535. Alexander, the Baxter, left a son, also called Alexander, who married Christian Burnett of Kinneskie, kinswoman to Burnett of Leys. He recorded his Arms at the Lyon Court in 1613 and became the founder of the family of Kingswells which he purchased in 1579.

The Lands of Kingswells, which are situated a few miles west of Aberdeen, were originally Crown property as they formed part of the great Stocket Forest, that happy hunting ground of the early Scottish kings. In the year 1319 king Robert the Bruce (1306–1329) gifted to the citizens of Aberdeen the whole of the Stocket Forest in recompense for their loyalty to the royal cause. From this gift emerged the Common Good Fund of Aberdeen.

In 1551 the Magistrates of the city evolved a plan for feuing the Freedom Lands in small estates at ridiculously low feu-duties—the feuars being none other than the Magistrates themselves. In this way, many of the burgesses of that time founded their family estates which, as time went on, yielded a handsome and ever increasing return to them and their heirs. Land speculation is obviously nothing new. In such a manner, the Lands of Kingswells were acquired by John Arthur, Burgess of Aberdeen, who did not live long to enjoy his possession for he died shortly afterwards. His son disposed of the property to the above-mentioned Alexander Jaffray.

Alexander Jaffray, 1st of Kingswells, died in 1627 and was succeeded by his son Alexander who, like his father and grandfather, took a keen interest in the business and civic life of Aberdeen, holding the office of Provost for three terms. He married Magdalen Erskine of Pittodrie by whom he had a family of fifteen, the eldest son Alexander becoming the 3rd Jaffray laird of Kingswells. He was by far the most distinguished member of the famous family.

Alexander Jaffray, 3rd of Kingswells, was born at Aberdeen in July, 1614. He was educated at the burgh Grammar School and later at the village schools of Banchory in Kincardineshire and at Pittodrie in Aberdeenshire, where he does not appear to have made much progress. At the age of seventeen, he entered Marischal College, Aberdeen, where, as he said himself "having staid a short time in the College, and profited as little" he gave up his studies—and married the Principal's daughter, Jean Dun. Shortly after his marriage Alexander Jaffray set out to see the world, travelling to France where he stayed some time. Returning to Aberdeen in 1636, he settled down to manage the family estate and take his place in the life of the community.

A man of singular ability, Alexander Jaffray was twice Provost of Aberdeen—in 1649 and again in 1651. His energies, however, were not confined to Aberdeen alone, for he was a member of the Scottish Parliament and was one of the Commissioners sent to the Hague to treat with Charles II (1630–1685). He was present at the Battle of Dunbar where his horse was shot from under him and he was taken prisoner. Later, Alexander Jaffray became a close personal friend of Oliver Cromwell, but declined the offer of a Judgeship which the Protector pressed upon him.

One of the most interesting items belonging to Alexander Jaffray is his *Diary*. This fascinating manuscript was discovered in the library at Ury House, near Stonehaven, and published in 1833. Ury House—now demolished—is well-known as being the home of Robert Barclay, the 'Apologist for the Quakers' and it seems likely that, as the Jaffrays and the Barclays intermarried, the *Diary* was removed from Kingswells to Ury and never returned. In his *Diary*, Alexander Jaffray describes his varied life and religious experiences well as many facts concerning the times in which he lived. It is an invaluable work to Quakers and historians alike.

Originally a staunch Covenanter, Alexander Jaffray embraced the tenets of the Quaker faith in 1662, in consequence of which he suffered much at the hands of his former colleagues. His continued persecution and failing health compelled him to retire from public life and he spent his declining years in the seclusion of Kingswells. Jaffray died on 7th July, 1673, and was laid to rest in the beautifully situated burial-ground on his estate. The practice of erecting headstones was not then considered compatible with Quaker beliefs, so that today the actual resting-place of this distinguished man can only be surmised. The burial-ground at Kingswells was exclusively used by the Quakers until 1838 when it fell into disuse. Few indeed know of its existence.

For several generations the Quaker interest continued at Kingswells where Alexander Jaffray had provided a Meeting

House for their use. In the grounds of Kingswells House a beautifully carved stone may still be seen bearing the inscription from 1. Peter ii. 5.

O. LORD. MAK. US
LYVELLYE. STONIS
OF. THY. ETERNAL
BUILDING. DEO. GLORIA.

In all probability this is the only relic of the Kingswells Meeting House as the building was demolished many years ago to make way for modern improvements.

Of the later Jaffrays of Kingswells little is known but their interest in the property remained until 1854 when Isabella Sarah Jaffray disposed of the family estate. One cannot, however, visit Kingswells and its immediate environs without becoming acutely conscious of the early Jaffrays for their devotion to their faith can be felt down the centuries.

11

Auchinhove's 'Houff'

"I love to loose myself in a mystery"—Browne.

One Saturday afternoon in the summer of 1963, while walking over one of the less frequented parts of Deeside—that delightful area between the parishes of Coull and Lumphanan—I stopped to admire the view, a stretch of flat countryside almost circular in form and surrounded by low hills. Obviously, the region had originally been marshland but centuries of toil had drained and cleared it and the land was now under cultivation. In the centre of the area were the remains of what appeared to be a small mound, its flat-topped summit rising some twenty feet above its surroundings. Part of it had recently been excavated, for the fresh yellow sand showed up clearly against the lush green of the crops. A closer inspection seemed the obvious thing to do.

The excavations had uncovered the fragmentary remains of some early building work formed of rough-hewn surface gatherings. Scattered around the foundations were a number of bones—human bones, I suspected, and before long I had picked up six coffin handles and some fragments of coffin boards. My next discovery was a human skull, startlingly white in the summer sunlight, and I wondered as I collected the items for further examination, what story lay behind my 'find'.

The first clue was provided by the 6″ Ordnance Survey Map of the district (LXXXII). The mounded site was marked *'Houff'*—an old Scots word for burial place. Of course my macabre discoveries proved this to be correct but the mystery

PLATE 11

(a) The partly excavated 'Houff' of Auchinhove.

(b) Lumphanan Church.

PLATE 12

(a) The second Mar Lodge on the *dail mor* circa 1750.

(b) The present Mar Lodge as designed and built by Alexander Marshall Mackenzie. The verandas have since been removed.

PLATE 13

No. 142 King Street, Aberdeen, the dignified building designed and
built by John Smith, City Architect, for his own occupation. It is now
occupied by the Boilermakers Social Recreation Club.

PLATE 14

No. 15 Guestrow, the birthplace of Archibald Simpson, architect. It was demolished in the Guestrow clearance scheme.

remained—whose burial place was it and why in this out-of-the-way place?

A search into the records of ownership revealed that in the late 14th century the land belonged to a family called Thomson, of whom little is known beyond the name of their property—Auchinhove (Gaelic: *Ach' an taoibh*—'field of the side'). About the year 1445, Elizabeth, daughter and heiress of Thomson of Auchinhove, married Robert Duguid and thereafter for upwards of three hundred years, the lands remained in the Duguids' possession. They were a family with an interesting history.

Robert Duguid and his wife Elizabeth Thomson had an only son Robert who succeeded to the maternal estates, confirmation of ownership being granted by James III in 1470. This Robert, 2nd of Auchinhove, married Agnes, daughter of Alexander Forbes, 4th of Brux, and their son, also called Robert, succeeded to Auchinhove *circa* 1500 as its 3rd laird. He married a daughter of Alexander Irvine, 6th of Drum, by whome he had a son William.

Robert Duguid, 3rd of Auchinhove, lived at a difficult time in history. Scotland was then at the crossroads—it had to choose between France and Catholicism or England and the Reformation. In consequence, the Roman Catholic families in the north-east began to consolidate and in 1536, in common with a number of other lairds, Robert Duguid entered into a bond of manrent with the most powerful Catholic nobleman in the area, George Gordon, 4th Earl of Huntly. This manrent bound the laird of Auchinhove, during Huntly's lifetime and his own, to take part in all the Earl's 'actions and quarrels against whatsumever person, state or dignity within the realm of Scotland or without, our Sovereign Lord's Highness only being excepted'. Among the witnesses to this bond was Duguid's near neighbour Nicol Ross of Auchlossan. However, Robert Duguid died the following year—in 1537—while Huntly survived until 1562 to die of a stroke following his capture on the tragic battlefield of Corrichie on the Hill o' Fare.

William Duguid, 4th of Auchinhove, married three times—first with Janet, daughter of John Leslie, 8th baron of Balquhain; second with Janet, daughter of William Forbes, 6th of Pitsligo; and third with his neighbour Agnes Ross of Auchlossan whose name figures prominently in the Witchcraft Trials of 1597. It would appear that Agnes, Lady Auchinhove, died of a mysterious illness which was traced back to the evening when she visited the Mill of Auchinhove. Before leaving the Mill, she bought a shoulder of mutton and proceeded to the home of her neighbour Beatrix Robbie, where she decided to stay overnight. Beatrix cooked the mutton and before retiring Lady Auchinhove ate some for her supper. During the night, however, she suddenly became unwell and the illness continued for some months 'ane half of the day burning like a fyrie furnace, the other half melting away in ane caul sweyt'. Eventually, the unfortunate Lady Auchinhove died in great pain. Beatrix Robbie and her mother Margaret Ogg were immediately suspected of witchcraft and committed for trial. A certificate was furnished by the Rev John Ross, parish minister of Lumphanan, categorically stating that the mutton had been bewitched by Robbie and Ogg and had caused the illness and death of Agnes, Lady Auchinhove, consequently both women were tried and found guilty of witchcraft. Margaret Ogg was burnt at the stake in Aberdeen while her daughter Beatrix Robbie was banished.

William Duguid, 4th of Auchinhove, appears to have died before 1593 and was succeeded by his son Robert. While still a youth, Robert married Janet, daughter of Robert Forbes, 5th of Echt, but in 1583, on account of his adultery with Elizabeth Mitchell—he was divorced. Subsequently, he married Marjory, daughter of Alexander Gordon, 4th of Abergeldie, but as both their families were Roman Catholics, the reformed Church of

Scotland refused to recognise the legality of the union and declared the two sons illegitimate. Auchinhove appealed to the king and in 1589 James VI issued a Royal decree legalising the marriage and Duguid's two sons—William, who succeeded to Auchinhove as its 6th laird, and Robert who eventually settled in Poland.

William Duguid succeeded his father as 6th laird of Auchinhove in 1614 and it would appear he had rather an adverse time. His first problem came in 1634 when John, 20th Earl of Mar, took an action of reduction against him, maintaining that the lands of Auchinhove were part of the Earldom of Mar and that its lairds were his vassals. Duguid pleaded that Auchinhove had always been held direct from the Crown consequently Mar had no legal claim over it. The case went in Duguid's favour and shortly after—no doubt as a precautionary measure—he had his properties erected into a free barony. William Duguid next became the unhappy victim of the notorious outlaw Patrick Macgregor. Better known as 'Gilderoy', he and his gang had settled in Cromar, their hide-out being the cave at Burn o' Vat, near Dinnet. From this remote spot, they terrorised the entire countryside, pillaging and burning any homestead in their path. Eventually, Auchinhove became their target and William Duguid was held to ransom in his own house—200 merks being demanded for his release. History is silent as to whether the ransom money was ever paid but in 1658 'Gilderoy' and his gang were captured by Sir William Forbes, 1st baronet of Craigievar, conveyed to Edinburgh, tried, found guilty and hanged. William Duguid married Margaret, daughter of Robert Forbes, 1st of Barnes—cadet of Monymusk, by whom he had a son Francis who succeeded to Auchinhove on his father's death in 1656.

Of Francis Duguid, 7th of Auchinhove, very little is known except that his wife was Elizabeth Seton of Meldrum; he had a charter from Charles II in 1673 under the Great Seal confirming Auchinhove as a barony; and had an only son Francis who succeeded him on his death in 1675. However, as we shall see, tradition has more to say about the 7th laird than recorded history.

Francis Duguid, 8th of Auchinhove, made a break with family tradition. In 1664 he became a student at King's College, Old Aberdeen, and subsequently was appointed one of the Commissioners to compile the *List of Pollable Persons in Aberdeenshire (1696)*. Oddly enough, the name of his wife is not recorded but she bore him seven children, the eldest son Robert succeeding to Auchinhove on his father's death in 1698. The following year, Robert married Teresa Leslie, 3rd daughter of Patrick, Count Leslie, 15th baron of Balquhain, and their son Patrick Duguid who in 1731 succeeded to Auchinhove as its 10th laird, subsequently succeeded to Balquhain as its 21st baron.

Patrick Duguid, usually referred to as Peter, was an ardent Jacobite and as a boy played a minor part in the unfortunate rising of 1715. However, on account of his youth, no proceedings were taken against him. In 1731, he married Isabella Dickson by whom he had three sons and a daughter, all of whom died in infancy. His wife died before 1740 for in that year he married Amelia, daughter of John Irvine, 8th of Kingcausie, who bore him eleven children, the fourth son John succeeding to Auchinhove on the death of his father in 1777. Peter Duguid took up arms for Prince Charles in 1745 and was most active in raising funds for the Jacobite cause. He was present at the battle of Inverurie—where he was wounded— and at Culloden. After the collapse of the Rising, Duguid returned to Deeside to find Auchinhove occupied by Hanoverian troops under the notorious Captain MacHardy. He was therefore obliged to 'lurk' on the neighbouring Hill of Coull while his wife and family remained at Auchinhove living in a state of constant anxiety as MacHardy was a man of very uncertain temperament. Tradition tells that one day the Captain suddenly dragged the five-year-old James Duguid from his box-bed and ordered him to cry "Hurrah! for King George", but young James was a lad of spirit and equal to the occasion. He promptly replied "Na faith sodjer, I'm a Prince's man". Eventually, Captain MacHardy gave up the hunt for Peter Duguid and one night without warning, ordered his soldiers to burn Auchinhove. Amelia Duguid and her children were fortunate enough to escape by a window while Peter watched the destruction of his home from a nearby hill. In connection with the Jacobite laird of Auchinhove there is a fascinating story. In 1760 a curious discovery was made by two herd boys near Roadside of Sunnybrae, not far from Auchinhove—a horde of Queen Anne shillings valued at £100. This was believed to be part of a fortune of 50,000 merks—Jacobite funds—concealed in a riding boot, carried from Auchinhove by the laird's man and hidden lest it fall into enemy hands. Unfortunately, the man was killed—and the location of the treasure died with him. Peter Duguid's second wife died in 1762 and he married for a third time—his cousin Eliza Grant. He was pardoned in 1775 for the part he played in the '45 and died two years later when his fourth son John succeeded as 11th laird of Auchinhove.

It seems unlikely that Auchinhove was ever rebuilt after its destruction by Captain MacHardy's troops in 1746 and today only its fragmentary ruins remain to remind posterity of the Duguid family. It appears to have been built by the 7th laird about the year 1670 and was a simple, stone-built tower-house typical of the period. It was, of course, the Duguid's second 'castle' their earlier stronghold lying about half-a-mile to the north. This first 'castle' belonged to the type of stronghold known as a 'motte'—a structure of earthwork and timber surrounded by extensive marshlands. It is possible that the 'motte' was built by the Thomsons and passed to the Duguids who lived there until the erection of the new house of Auchinhove.

Now to return to my 'find', from which developed the researches into the Duguid family of Auchinhove. The conical mound where the relics were found was, of course, none other than the 'motte'—the early stronghold of the Thomsons and the Duguids. The report on the skeletal remains revealed that the skull—of unusual size—was of a powerfully built man as were some of the bones. A number of bones were identified as belonging to a small man of slender build, while the remainder proved to be those of a small woman. Obviously, there had been three interments on the 'motte'—two men and a woman. The iron coffin handles, ingeniously hinged for carrying the coffin on spokes, were hand-wrought of a type made locally during the 17th century.

The three interments on the 'motte'—later known as the 'Houff'—remained a mystery, for the burial vault of the Duguid family of Auchinhove, heritors in the parish, was in Lumphanan kirk-yard.

Occasionally, when recorded history fails, it is useful to recourse to local tradition, for as the old Scots proverb has it *'there's aye some water whaur the stirkie droons'*. In this instance, tradition tells that one of the Duguid lairds had a bitter feud with his neighbour Ross of Auchlossan and when on his death-bed Auchinhove expressed the wish to be buried on his own land—it would be a humiliation to carry him through enemy territory to reach the family vault in Lumphanan kirk-yard. Again tradition asserts that Auchinhove's last wish was implemented and pinpoints him as being the 7th laird—Francis Duguid. It tells too that he, his mother Margaret Forbes of Barnes, and Father Seton, the family priest, all died within six days of each other at Auchinhove in the year 1675. The sad story is recounted in an obscure poem seemingly written shortly after the unhappy events—

Epitaph on the Laird of Auchinhove, his Mother and Chaplain:
"In twice three days all under one same roof—
Priest, Laird, Old Lady, died at Auchinhuif.
Three such distinguished worthies death has snatched,
As in their stations rarely could be matched.
Of Seton's noble blood the Priest was come,
Who long the world had left ere it left him;
On orbs above his mind was fixed, and free
From earthly ties, so heavenly aye was he.
His life was chaste—religious—full of zeal,
Great pity 'twas he died, he lived so well.
Brave Auchinhuif, the Laird, lived wond'rous fast,
So next the Priest, he was the next that passed.
I'll style him man—man every inch—was man
For strength and manhood—match him if you can—
Man, both of head and heart and hand together—
Man, who feared God, and feared no other.
His faith called for the Priest before he dee;
Priest came in time, then stepped into eternity.
Such blessed example of his dying Priest,
Revived his soul with hopes to be the next,
And follow him who bravely led the way.
To eternal bliss—so just next very day
At self same hour, the Priest had then expired,
Brave Auchinhuif got what he most desired.
The Virtuous Lady spun out her vital thread
Eighty-one years, she, saint-like lived and died.
She wished no longer to outlive her son,
She got her wish five short days after him.
Thus buried lie those worthies three together—
The Priest, the Laird, and Lady, the Laird's mother.
May those they've laft to fill the vacant stage
Such worthies prove, and thus decore our age."
Truth, they say, is stranger than fiction. However, the

accidental discovery of the human remains on the abandoned 'motte' suggests that sometimes truth and fiction can both be equally strange!

12

Mar Lodge

*"The Present is the sum-total of the whole
Past"*—Thomas Carlyle.

Probably at no time in Scottish history has the social structure
of the country been so drastically changed as in the past fifty
years. Possibly not since the abortive Jacobite Risings have so
many great estates been torn apart and mansion-houses razed.

The number of great houses already destroyed in north-east
Scotland is quite staggering, but of the few which have survived, solely on account of their adaptation to some other use,
Mar Lodge is undoubtedly one of the most important. Twelve
miles west from Balmoral Castle, it was in its heyday a
fabulous royal residence.

The present Mar Lodge—now a hotel—is the fourth of the
name and the third to occupy the same site on the *dail
mor*—the 'great haugh'—on the north bank of the River Dee,
four miles above Braemar in Aberdeenshire. It was from this
dail mor that the first lodge derived its name Dalmore. This
lodge was built about the beginning of the 16th century and
stood in the very heart of the Royal Forest of Mar, the extensive hunting-ground of the early Celtic kings.

The first lairds of Dalmore were Mackenzies from Kintail in
Wester Ross. Mackenzie of Kintail was a close friend of James
IV (1488–1513) and when Mackenzie was killed in a skirmish
with the Buchanans of Athole, the king, out of regard for his
friend, granted to Kintail's elder natural son Kenneth, the *dail
mor* by the River Dee in the Royal Forest of Mar. Here
Kenneth Mackenzie built the first Mar Lodge—then called

Dalmore—and eventually married 'the girl next door' Beatrix Farquharson of Invercauld, a daughter of the redoubtable Findla Mor by his second wife Beatrix Garden of Banchory.

For over two centuries the Mackenzies remained at Dalmore where their stirring deeds are recalled in local legends. However, the Mackenzies' participation in the Jacobite Rising of 1715 brought dool and destruction to the family and Dalmore was forfeited to the Crown. With their feudal superior, John Erskine, 24th Earl of Mar—'Bobbin' Jock'—both Kenneth Mackenzie and his son James were present at the raising of the Jacobite standard at Braemar, the latter figuring prominently throughout the unhappy campaign.

In 1720 Dalmore was purchased by the Lords Grange and Dun and in 1730 the property was acquired by William Duff, M.P. for Banffshire. He was a son of William Duff of Dipple in Moray—a very remarkable character, merchant, banker and money-lender—who claimed descent from the ancient Earls of Fife on somewhat obscure grounds but whose son eventually became Earl of Fife in the Irish Peerage.

It would seem that the original lodge of Dalmore—probably a small fortified tower-house—had fallen into disrepair and in consequence a new house was built *circa* 1750 on the *dail mor*. Contemporary drawings show this to have been a simple rectangular building of three storeys with low flanking wings. With the completion of this new house, the original name Dalmore was dropped and Mar Lodge substituted.

From time immemorial the *dail mor* had been liable to serious flooding from the River Dee, but the 'Muckle Spate' of 1829 proved calamitous. The effects of this fantastic spate are still to be seen in the district for it altered the course of several streams and caused extensive damage to property.

Mar Lodge was no exception and it was largely due to the damage done by the 'Muckle Spate' that the third lodge came to be built on the south side of the River Dee high above the *dail mor*. The new lodge, subsequently called Corriemulzie Cottage, stood on the lower slopes of the rugged Creag an Fhithich (Craig of the Raven) in the centre of a vast pine forest. Of small dimensions, Corriemulzie Cottage was built in the Swiss chalet style and here the Duffs resided during the 'Scottish Season' in preference to living at old Mar Lodge. In 1852 Queen Victoria (1837–1901) attended an open-air ball at Corriemulzie Cottage and in her *Journal* graphically describes the highlight of that memorable evening—a reel danced by brawny Highlanders carrying torches.

The Scots fixation to an old site is, of course, traditional, and when in 1895 it was decided to build a new Mar Lodge, the *dail mor* was selected—but with every precaution to safeguard it against the possibility of another 'Muckle Spate'.

The architect selected for the new lodge—the present Mar Lodge—was Alexander Marshall Mackenzie of Aberdeen, but the style of the new building was dictated by his client's wife—H.R.H. Princess Louise—who had a penchant for Elizabethan architecture. Thus the fourth Mar Lodge was built in this picturesque English style of architecture, Queen Victoria laying the foundation stone on October 15th, 1895. The familiar Victoria Bridge over the River Dee giving access to Mar Lodge is a reminder of this historic occasion.

But to return to the Duffs. The origin of the Clan Macduff is lost in the mists of antiquity. However, tradition tells that the Macduff who slew Maelbetha—Shakespeare's *Macbeth*—in the woods of Lumphanan on Deeside—thus recapturing the throne of Scotland for the royal House of Dunkeld—was the 8th Thane of Fife. Macduff is said to have married Beatrix Banquo, daughter of the Thane of Lochaber and, it is believed, was created 1st Earl of Fife by Malcolm Canmore in 1057.

As the 'restorers' of the House of Dunkeld, the chiefs of the Clan Macduff were vested with the hereditary honour of seating the King of Scots in the royal chair at his Coronation, a duty which they faithfully discharged down the centuries. However, with the advent of Robert the Bruce (1306–1329) came difficulty. Duncan Macduff, 3rd Earl of Fife, was a supporter of Baliol while his sister Isabel had married John Comyn, 3rd Earl of Buchan, Bruce's sworn enemy. The situation was therefore an extremely delicate one, yet the Countess of Buchan—despite hostility from her brother and her husband—rode to Scone and at Bruce's Coronation performed the hereditary duty of her family. Unhappily, the brave Countess of Buchan was captured soon afterwards and, on the express orders of Edward I of England, conveyed to Berwick Castle where she was imprisoned in an iron cage for seven long years.

The 4th Earl of Fife was Gillmichael Macduff who died in 1139. He had two sons, Duncan, who succeeded his father as 5th Earl, and Hugo Macduff, ancestor of the present Earl of Wemyss. The old Earldom of Fife terminated in 1353 on the death of Duncan Macduff the 12th Earl who, after an adventurous life in the service of David II, died without issue. The 12th Earl's daughter Isabel Macduff, was married four times but had no children. Her four husbands successively claimed the Earldom of Fife but on her death in 1389 the title appears to have passed through a period of obscurity. However, by the year 1425 the Earldom of Fife had reverted to the Crown and over three centuries were to pass before it was revived.

It is doubtful if evidence will ever be forthcoming to prove any link between the old Earls of Fife and the present line, but it is possible, of course, that there was some tie through one of the many cadet branches of the Macduff family. The present line derives from David Duff of Muldavit in Banffshire who married Agnes de Camera—the old name for Chalmers. David Duff is said to have been descended from a younger son of the 5th or 6th Earl of Fife but there appears to be no evidence to support this claim. However, from the Muldavit family came Adam Duff of Clunybeg who was born in 1590. Adam Duff's grandson was the already mentioned William Duff of Dipple whose fantastic career founded the family fortunes. William's father—Alexander Duff of Keithmore—recounts a spectral visitation at William's birth in 1653—"of ane greene ladye who approached Willie's cradle and stretched forth her hand over it". Whether this supernatural incident had any effect on William's career we shall never know but he certainly amassed a very considerable fortune. It is interesting to note that Duff of Dipple's banking-house still stands in Elgin's High Street and is one of the most fascinating buildings in Scotland. William Duff of Dipple died in 1722 and was succeeded by his son William, the only one of his sons to survive their father.

William Duff—'a man of extraordinary good sense'—was more scholar than business man, yet with the money he had inherited he added to the family estates and in 1735 was created Lord Braco by George II (1727–1760) and in 1759 became Viscount Macduff and Earl of Fife in the Irish Peerage. He died in 1763 and was succeeded by his second son James whose wife Lady Dorothea Sinclair, only child of the 9th Earl of Caithness, brought him a dowry of £40,000. James's younger brother Alexander succeeded to the title becoming 3rd Earl of Fife. He also married well and through his wife Mary Skene, eldest daughter of George Skene of that ilk, eventually added the Lands of Skene to the Duff properties. He also added another Deeside estate—Balmoral, which he purchased in 1798 from the Farquharsons. Alexander Duff was succeeded by his eldest son James and he, in turn, by his nephew James Duff who thus became 5th Earl of Fife.

James Duff, 5th Earl of Fife, was the eldest son of General Sir Alexander Duff of Delgaty. He was born in Edinburgh in 1814 and received his education there. He married Lady Agnes Hay, second daughter of the 16th Earl of Erroll by his wife

Lady Elizabeth Fitzclarence, daughter of William IV and Mrs Jordan.

In 1852, the 5th Earl of Fife disposed of one of his Deeside properties to H.R.H. Prince Albert—the estate of Balmoral—which thereafter became Queen Victoria's Scottish home. James Duff died in 1879 and was succeeded by his only son Alexander who in 1889, on his marriage with H.R.H. The Princess Louise, eldest daughter of King Edward VII (1901–1910) was elevated to the Dukedom of Fife. This marriage brought two daughters—T.H. Princess Alexandra and Princess Maud. Princess Alexandra—Duchess of Fife in her own right on the death of her father in 1912—married H.R.H. Prince Arthur of Connaught and Strathearn, grandson of Queen Victoria, and their son Alastair, Earl of Macduff, would have succeeded but for his death while on active service in the Second World War. Princess Maud married Charles Carnegie, eldest son of Charles, 10th Earl of Southesk. Their son James, Master of Carnegie, succeeded to the Dukedom of Fife on his aunt's death in 1959.

With the death of H.H. Princess Arthur of Connaught, Duchess of Fife, Mar Lodge ceased to be a Royal residence. The future of the great mansion seemed uncertain and it was put on the market. Mar Lodge was subsequently purchased by the brothers John and Gerald Panchaud, Anglo-Swiss business men who envisaged it as an all-the-year-round holiday centre. The once fabulous Royal home thus became a people's playground and in this new role another chapter opened in its fascinating history.

13

Creators of the "Granite City"

"The great artist is the simplifier"—Amiel.

Thirty years ago Aberdeen and *The Granite City* were synonymous terms. Today, however, as the town rapidly develops along lines and in building materials similar to any other town in Great Britain, its Postal Code—AB—may eventually become its only distinguishing feature.

The earliest plan of Aberdeen is that of 1661. It shows a small, compact burgh, roughly triangular in form. Successive plans, covering the next hundred and forty years, show little change but by 1880 a definite move had been made to develop the town. On account of its situation, expansion could only take place to the north and west and accordingly two new streets were planned with the Castlegate—the civic centre from around 1290—as the focal point. By the formation of these two new streets—Union Street and King Street—the way opened for the creation of a new Aberdeen. Although by the year 1817 the town was rendered bankrupt by the grandiose scheme, it was in fact the dawn of a new era of immense opportunity and among those who grasped its full significance were two young men—John Smith (1781–1852) and Archibald Simpson (1790–1847). Both were Aberdonians, born and bred, and both were architects of unusual ability and vision—they were jointly the creators of 'The Granite City' tradition. There is no doubt, of course, that Smith and Simpson were exceptionally fortunate in 'getting in on the ground floor' of Aberdeen's development for, shortly before they commenced in practice, the first feus of the newly formed streets were put up for sale as *The Aberdeen Journal* (1806) reports—'We are happy to learn that on Saturday last, 5th February, a stance of 40 feet in front, on the south side of Union Street of this city, was purchased, by public roup, at an yearly feu-duty of £1:11/8d. per foot of front. This is the first stance in the street which has been offered to feu; and, immediately after the roup, 74 feet more next adjoining were purchased at the same rate of feu-duty'.

Smith commenced practice in 1805 while Simpson followed eight years later. Both men were to be professional rivals for the next thirty-four years and it is interesting to trace their respective backgrounds and subsequent careers which brought Aberdeen world-wide renown.

John Smith was born in Aberdeen in the year 1781. He was the son of a local mason, William Smith, the first of a very remarkable line of builders which continued through four generations. William was a man of exceptional abilities both in design and construction, as the few remaining examples of his work show, while his handling of dressed granite, then in the early stages of its development as a building stone, was far in advance of his rivals in the building trade. Known to his contemporaries as *'Sink 'em'*—his favourite expletive—William appears to have been a man of strong character, shrewd and sound in business, who lived for his family and his work. Apart from a few houses in Marischal Street, it is to be regretted that no complete list of his buildings has survived, while particulars of his life are lamentably few.

During his career as a builder in Aberdeen, William Smith had come to realise that what the burgh lacked were properly trained architects, the few who practised in the town being of the self-taught or dilettante type. Consequently, when his son John—who had attended the Grammar School and served an apprenticeship with his father as an operative mason—had

PLATE 15

John Brown, Queen Victoria's Highland Attendant, wearing the Balmoral tartan. The photograph was taken in 1855 by George Washington Wilson, Scotland's pioneer photographer.

PLATE 16

John Taylor (1580–1653), 'The Water Poet'.

PLATE 17

No. 61 Schoolhill, Aberdeen. The division of the window frames, stressing the horizontal lines of the building, was a break with tradition which eventually proved popular and was extensively used by Archibald Simpson.

PLATE 18

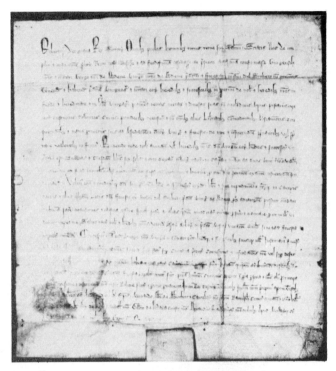

(a) Robert the Bruce's charter granted to the citizens of Aberdeen in 1319.

(b) 'Largo Tower', part of Sir Andrew Wood's stronghold in Fifeshire.

completed his practical training, he was sent off to London to study architecture. John appears to have been about twenty years old when he travelled to London by package boat from Aberdeen, but the names of the doyens of the architectural profession under whom he studied do not appear to have been recorded—indeed the reticence of the whole Smith family regarding their family life and professional activities is unfortunate, particularly today when their enormous influence and contribution to the city's architectural heritage is being freshly assessed.

In 1805 John Smith returned to Aberdeen—again by package boat, but this time during a period of great gales with heavy seas causing many wrecks. In a state of much anxiety, 'Sink 'em' Smith went to the pier-head to watch his son's homecoming and later recounted that at one point as 'the boatie' crossed the bar, he thought that "Johnnie an' a' his bonnie plannies frae London" would go down! Happily for posterity, fortune was on his side and later that year John Smith set up in business as an architect in Aberdeen.

John Smith's first commission—and the first building to be erected in Union Street west of Union Bridge—was a townhouse for Peter Milne of Crimmonmogate. Long known as the Royal Northern Club, it was, oddly enough, the first of Smith's works to be demolished—and one of his finest. Other work followed as his reputation as an architect increased. In 1824 he was appointed City Architect and Superintendent of Public Works, the first to hold this onerous office. It says much for Smith's abilities that he was able to tackle—in addition to his own professional commitments—the multifarious tasks which fell to him in his new official capacity, for his responsibilities included such items as the erection of public buildings and their maintenance, town-planning, construction work of various kinds, streets and roads, civil engineering, together with a seemingly endless output of reports—written in faultless script—on housing, bridges, quays, kilns, dams, mills, and farm buildings. The erection of the public gallows was another of his duties when occasion demanded.

John Smith married Margaret, only child of Colonel George Grant of Auchterblair in Banffshire—a hero of the Peninsular War. The first years of their married life were spent at No 20 Longacre—a street long since demolished. Now covered by the south wing of Marischal College, Longacre ran parallel to Queen Street, and here John Smith had his office. His practice increased and eventually he built for his own occupation—as home and business premises—No 142 King Street, the handsome, porticoed building now occupied by the Boilermakers Social Recreation Club, and from this address John Smith, his son and grandson continued to conduct their architectural practice for many years. About 1850, however, John Smith moved 'to the country'—to Rosebank, a pleasantly situated house which he built near Willowbank, the home of his close friend and business associate John Gibb (1776–1850), civil engineer. Smith's daughter Margaret Grant married Gibb's son Alexander. No longer 'in the country', Rosebank is part of a tenement block in Rosebank Place off the Hardgate, while Willowbank is now occupied by the Health Department of the Aberdeen Town Council.

The first ecclesiastical building to be erected by John Smith in Aberdeen was the North Parish Church in King Street—now the Arts Centre—built in 1831. Undoubtedly one of the most impressive buildings in the city, it was modelled on H. W. Inwood's St Pancras Church, London, itself inspired by the Erechthrion and the Temple of the Winds, Athens. Other Aberdeen churches to John Smith's credit include the South Parish Church in Belmont Street (1831), now the halls of West St Nicholas Church, St Clement's Church—'Fittie Kirk'—(1828), and the well-known Kirk of Nigg (1828). All three churches have a strong 'family likeness'.

By the turn of the century John Smith had designed and built a number of noteworthy public buildings in the city such as Advocates' Hall in Union Street (1838)—now the Queen's Cinema, the Blind Asylum in Huntly Street (1841), the Union Street facade to St Nicholas Churchyard (1830), and the Town Schools in Little Belmont Street (1840).

On Deeside, John Smith had been busy with a number of country houses—Banchory, Raemore and Learney, and he had made various additions to the old castle of Balmoral then leased to Sir Robert Gordon. However, on Sir Robert's sudden death, the lease was taken over by Queen Victoria who stayed at the castle for the first time in 1848. Consequently, in September of that year, *The Aberdeen Journal* reports—'We understand that John Smith Esq, architect, has received Her Majesty's command to attend at Balmoral today (16:9:1848) between the hours of one and three p.m. It may not be impertinent to assume that additions to the buildings are contemplated'. This was John Smith's first—and perhaps his only contact with Royalty, for it fell to his son William to design and build the present Balmoral Castle.

Perhaps John Smith's best-known work on Deeside is Morison's Suspension Bridge—the popular 'Shakkin' Briggie' at Cults—erected in 1836 and now almost derelict. It was one of several bridges designed by Smith—the list includes the Bridge of Don—and where these are built of stone, their parapets all bear the indelible stamp of John Smith—the ogee profiled coping in the Tudor tradition—which, with his penchant for this particular architectural style, earned for him the byname 'Tudor Johnnie'.

The long list of buildings designed by John Smith, not only in Aberdeen but all over the north-east corner, is indeed remarkable for any man to have tackled single-handed, yet it was said of him 'all went on under his own immediate inspection, so that he might in every case with truth say "let work bear witness" '. His unique influence on the architecture of north-east Scotland cannot be over-emphasised.

John Smith died on 22nd July, 1852 at his 'country house' Rosebank. He was buried in St Nicholas Churchyard where a dignified monument designed by his son marks the family vault. Shortly before his death he had taken into partnership his son William who, in turn, assumed as partner his son John. In 1887, however, John Smith died at the old home, 142 King Street, when his father selected as partner a former assistant, William Kelly, who not only upheld the fine tradition of the Smith family but in his own right added fresh laurels to the city's architectural reputation.

John Smith's professional rival was Archibald Simpson who was born at No 15 Guestrow, Aberdeen, on 4th May, 1790. His father, William Simpson, was a native of Kincardineshire who, in 1770, moved to Aberdeen where he joined his brother Joseph in taking over a clothier's business in Broad Street. The Simpsons prospered. Eventually they assumed as a partner John Whyte, a well-known magistrate, and thereafter the firm was styled Simpson and Whyte, a name long familiar to the Aberdeen public and indeed to the tailoring trade throughout the country.

In 1773 William Simpson married Barbara Dauney—sometimes spelt Downie—daughter of Francis Dauney, minister of Banchory-Ternan, Kincardineshire, and one suspects that this union was the fulfilment of a friendship formed before Simpson moved to Aberdeen. The Dauneys were a talented family. Dr Alexander Dauney, Barbara's brother, was an advocate and sheriff-substitute in Aberdeen, while another brother, William, was an architect of some repute. It was he who designed the Simpsons' house in the Guestrow *circa* 1786, a simple building with some interesting plasterwork and pine panelling, which was demolished in the 1930 clearances—the City Rates Department, St Nicholas House now occupies the site.

Archibald Simpson was the fourth son and the youngest of a family of nine. In 1800 he was sent to Aberdeen Grammar School where he remained for three years, a diligent but undistinguished pupil. The death of his mother in 1801 was a great shock to Archibald's sensitive nature and he felt his loss very keenly. In 1803 he passed into Marischal College intending to graduate in Arts but his father's death in 1804 necessitated his leaving college and he began the study of architecture.

Two factors appear to have drawn Archibald Simpson to the architectural profession. Firstly, the influence of his uncle William, and secondly his health. Never robust, Archibald had the added handicap of a deformed left arm—the result of an accident which had not received proper medical attention. He was not, however, apprenticed to his uncle but to James Massie, a well-known Aberdeen builder from whom he received a thoroughly practical training in building construction and the elements of architectural design.

In 1810 Archibald Simpson went to London where he entered the office of Robert Lugar (1773–1855), then at the height of his popularity as a 'Country Gentleman's Architect'. Lugar was the author of several works published in London between 1807 and 1828 and was a regular exhibitor at the Royal Academy of Arts. Although Simpson stayed only a year in Lugar's office, he appears to have been greatly influenced by his employer's work for many of Simpson's country houses and lodges bear a striking resemblance to Lugar's designs.

Wishing to broaden his experience, Simpson tried to find employment with some of the other important architects of the day—Sir John Soane (1753–1837), George Dance (1741–1825), Robert Smirke (1781–1867) and Joseph Gwilt (1784–1863) of 'Encyclopedia' fame, but without success. This was not surprising for in those days influence meant everything and young Simpson had very little.

It was a difficult period for Simpson and little wonder he became despondent. His letters home at this time disclose his feeling of intense frustration and when, in his extremity, he sought the advice of Samuel Peyps Cockerel (1754–1827), the celebrated architect's counsel only added to his despair. He was advised to give up the study of architecture as it was 'a hopeless profession without a connection of consequence'. How much poorer Aberdeen would have been if Simpson had accepted Cockerel's dictum!

Whether it was due to his Scottish thrawness or an inner knowledge of his own potentiality that dissuaded him from acting on Cockerel's advice we shall never know, but Archibald Simpson resolved to continue his studies and went abroad—to France and Italy, returning to Aberdeen in the year 1813, determined to set up in practice as an architect. At first he worked from his old home No 15 Guestrow, but work was slow to come in. It was a trying period for the young architect but he found relief in music—he and his brother Alexander revived the Aberdeen Musical Society and throughout his life, until the Society broke up in 1838, he was an enthusiastic member, playing the violin.

While resident in London, Simpson had prepared plans for two buildings in Aberdeen—Union Buildings (17–21 Union Street) and Union Chambers (46–50 Union Street) built in 1813–14. Simpson's first commission from his office in the Guestrow came in 1815—a mansion-house at Putachie on Donside for James Ochoncar, 18th Lord Forbes—the present Castle Forbes. The same year Simpson was awarded the commission for St Andrew's Episcopal Church in King Street—since raised to the status of Cathedral—which he gained in competition with his rivals John Smith and James Young, architects, of London. Simpson appears to have had little feeling for Gothic architecture and although his work in this style is always competent, it is frequently rather dull.

Other work followed and Simpson was obliged to open an office at 130 Union Street—the east corner of Belmont Street. However, in 1826, an unfortunate fire in the building destroyed all his drawings and he moved his office—and house—to 8 Belmont Street. Subsequently, Simpson acquired premises at 22 Crown Street—where the General Post Office now stands—but later moved to Bon-Accord Square having his house at No 15 and his office at No 1. Finally he settled at No 1 East Craibstone Street.

By the year 1820 Archibald Simpson was well on the way to success. It was now abundantly clear that a new Aberdeen was emerging after centuries of stagnation. No longer a small county burgh, it was rapidly becoming a busy commercial centre with an ever-increasing population. Accordingly, new housing areas had to be planned and developed and it is perhaps in this particular field that Simpson's abilities are seen at their best.

Space does not permit of a detailed description of Simpson's grand vision for a new Aberdeen—a 'silver city by the sea'—with wide streets, dignified squares and crescents and stately terraces—enough to say he had complete mastery of both architecture and town-planning, a rare combination. Had his successors followed the course he set, Aberdeen might easily have been one of the finest cities in the country.

Fortunately a few Simpson-planned streets remain tolerably intact, such as East and West Craibstone Street, Bon-Accord Square and Crescent, part of Crown Street, part of Springbank Terrace and Marine Terrace. His inspired plan for the development of the west end—Albyn Place, Rubislaw Terrace, Queen's Terrace and the neighbouring streets—were never carried out and it is to be regretted that, when development did take place after Simpson's death, his scheme was dropped in favour of a very commonplace layout.

By the year 1827 Archibald Simpson had established

himself and his professional services were much in demand. At this time he was working in several counties—Aberdeenshire, Banffshire, Bute, Forfarshire, Kincardineshire, Midlothian and Moray.

As Simpson became established he became less pliable and, like so many artists, resented direction. Disputes with his clients were frequent and, although he could handle the hard, crystalline granite as no man has done since, he found the Aberdeen mentality infinitely more intractable. Archibald Simpson was not always right in his opinions but they were sincerely held. In 1835 he advocated—and unfortunately was allowed to carry out his wishes—the demolition of the East Church of St Nicholas, the freestone choir of the 15th-century 'Toun's Kirk', erecting in its place the uninspired granite building we know today. This, and his proposal to face the ancient Bridge of Dee with fine-axed granite—happily prevented by his rival John Smith—are two of several 'black spots' in Simpson's otherwise brilliant career. Like so many of the present-day architects, Simpson disliked being hampered in his work by existing buildings, yet it is sad to think of the number of fine medieval buildings he demolished to make way for his Classic style mansions. The wheel has now made full turn and today many of Simpson's buildings are being demolished—usually for the same reason.

The 1840s saw Simpson busy with another group of country houses and with some larger schemes including the New Market, recently demolished. Miss Emslie's Institution (later called the High School for Girls and now Harlaw Academy) was built in 1840 and the North of Scotland Bank in Castle Street in the same year.

It was becoming obvious that Archibald Simpson was overworking—the long list of buildings to his credit is sufficient proof. His last work was the Union Bank at Lerwick—a small commission but obviously inspired by his first chief, Robert

Lugar. It was completed in 1846.

On 3rd March, 1847, Simpson attended a meeting of the Aberdeen Police Commissioners—a body to which he had been elected in 1839 to represent No 9 Ward of the city—when another great street development was discussed. A few days later, tired and unwell, he left by coach for Durham on business and when he returned to Aberdeen Simpson was a very sick man. A few days later, erysipelas developed and he died at his home in East Craibstone Street on 23rd March, 1847. He never married.

Like his professional rival John Smith, Archibald Simpson was laid to rest in St Nicholas Churchyard where his grave is marked by a simple granite slab. Simpson's business was carried on by his former assistant James Matthews (1820–1898) who was later joined by Alexander Marshall Mackenzie (1848–1933), the architect of Marischal College.

Thus the vision of a 'Granite City' begun by John Smith and Archibald Simpson continued with their successors until after the Second World War (1939–1945) when the break with tradition commenced.

14

Highland Attendant

"Beware of a half truth; you may have got hold of the wrong half."

A great deal has been written about John Brown, Queen Victoria's Highland Attendant. There is no doubt that much of what has been written is based on hearsay, liberally embellished, so that the fantastic figure of John Brown as presented to the public today is a complete travesty, a Sassenach's burlesque of what he imagines this colourful Highland character should be even to a Glasgow accent.

It has been said that, while history repeats itself, historians—and fiction writers—repeat each other. Never was this more true than in the case of John Brown's biographers who, time and again, present the same set of 'facts' about him, his personal appearance, his character and his family—most of them quite fictitious.

John Brown's background is an intensely interesting one for his family ties link him with several of the great and powerful Highland Clans. Brown entered the Royal Service in 1851 and although Queen Victoria knew something of her Attendant's background, it was not until 1865 that she instituted a search into Brown's ancestry. The initial work for this was carried out by Her Majesty's Commissioner at Balmoral, Dr Andrew Robertson of Hopewell, whose neatly written *Memorandum* on the subject is of unusual interest. Dr Robertson was related to John Brown and was therefore in an excellent position to undertake the necessary research work.

It will be remembered that it was Queen Victoria's intention to write the life-story of her Highland Attendant. This was to be the third volume of her *Our Life in the Highlands*. It is a matter of history that this volume was abandoned under pressure from The Establishment—notably from the Church and certain members of the Royal Family. The wisdom of this decision to abandon publication is open to question—especially in the light of subsequent events.

John Brown's family tree is a remarkable document. From both his parents he derived from Jacobite stock—his father's family coming from Angus, his mother's from Rothiemurchus. Perhaps it was John Brown's Jacobite ancestry that aroused Queen Victoria's interest in her Attendant's family tree for she regarded herself—and with sound reason—as the representative of the ancient Royal House of Stuart. Whether John Brown agreed with Her Majesty's claim is a moot point but it certainly appears to have been a perennial and lively topic of conversation between the Queen and her Attendant for a great many years.

John Brown's paternal grandfather was Donald Brown who, about the year 1770, had crossed the Grampians by the Capel Mounth Pass from Angus into Aberdeenshire. For generations, the Browns had been tenants of the Earls of Airlie, farming the land around the Kirriemuir district. In 1745, however, Donald Brown's father and uncles—all of them ardent Jacobites—had joined Lord Ogilvie's Forfarshire Regiment, served all through the Rising, and had taken part in the Battle of Culloden. On the disbandment of the Forfarshire Regiment, the Browns, like so many of their fellow-countrymen, were obliged to 'lurk' near their homes but were powerless to protect them from the repeated plunderings and burnings by the Government troops. It was a time of great hardship and much uncertainty, thus, in order to ease the family burdens, young Donald Brown resolved to leave home and make a way for himself in another area—the Crathie district of Deeside. Eventually, Donald

Brown was fortunate enough to obtain a lease of the small-holding of Rhinachat on the Monaltrie Estate—the property of that redoubtable Jacobite, Francis Farquharson, better known on Deeside as 'Baron Ban'. Once established at Rhinachat, Donald Brown married Janet Shaw, second daughter of James Shaw, Crathienaird, by whom he had a family of six sons including John Brown—subsequently of Bush—the father of Queen Victoria's Highland Attendant.

In his *Memorandum* to Queen Victoria—dated 2nd June, 1865—Dr Andrew Robertson says in referring to John Brown's ancestry, that John "is every inch a Shaw" and that the "qualities which have recommended him to Your Majesty" were largely derived from his maternal great-grandfather James Shaw whom Dr Robertson describes as "remarkably hand-some, of a warm generous disposition, possessing all the high and chivalrous feelings of the Highland gentleman, displaying much shrewdness and possessing a high intelligence." John Brown's descent from the Shaws is therefore significant.

James Shaw, already referred to, was descended from Shaw Mor 'of the buck tooth', first of the Rothiemurchus line. The 3rd Shaw of Rothiemurchus was Alasdair Ciar whose fourth son Farquhar settled in Aberdeenshire. This Farquhar's son, Donald, married Isobel Stewart of Invercauld, and their son, Finla Mor, was the first Farquharson of Invercauld. The Shaws and the Farquharsons were thus related and this relationship was brought closer when James Shaw of Tullochgrue in Rothiemurchus married Beatrix Farquharson of Invercauld, settling on the Farquharson lands on upper Deeside. They were the direct ancestors of James Shaw, the maternal great-grandfather of John Brown, Queen Victoria's Attendant.

From the same line of Shaws came Janet Shaw, the wife of Dr Andrew Robertson, Her Majesty's Commissioner at Balmoral, and Ellen Shaw whose son, Sir John Alexander

Macdonald, was Her Majesty's Prime Minister in Canada. Sir John's wife Isabel Clark—also of Shaw descent—was created a Peeress in her own right on her husband's death in 1891.

As already mentioned, Donald Brown and Janet Shaw had a family of six sons. Of these, John Brown, farmer in Bush, Crathie, married Margaret Leys, daughter of Charles Leys, blacksmith in Aberarder, by whom he had a family of eleven—nine sons and two daughters. The second son was John Brown, the Queen's Highland Attendant. He was born at Crathienaird on 8th December, 1826, entered the Royal Household in 1851 and after thirty-two years of devoted service to Queen Victoria, died in the Clarence Tower, Windsor Castle, on 27th March 1883. His mortal remains were brought home to Deeside and lie in the quiet little kirk-yard at Crathie surrounded by his kinsfolk—the Browns, the Leys, the Clarks, the Shaws and the Farquharsons. Over his grave is the headstone erected by his grateful Sovereign. It bears the words by Tennyson—

> "That friend on whose fidelity you count,
> that friend given to you by circumstances over which
> you have no control,
> was God's own gift."

15

Early Tourist

" 'Tis a mad world, my masters"—John Taylor.

According to popular belief, Royal Deeside—that beautiful and romantic region of Aberdeenshire—was the 'discovery' of Queen Victoria. It is true, of course, that before Victoria's reign the upper valley of the Dee was a remote region where time stood still, yet it was not altogether unknown for, out of the past, there emerges from time to time, descriptions of Deeside penned by observant visitors—vivid, personal, impressions—unlike so much that is written today with the express purpose of 'selling' the valley to the tourist—down to the last Highland souvenir, frequently made in Japan.

One of these early 'tourists' was John Taylor who visited Deeside in 1618 and left to posterity his remarkable and highly entertaining diary—the *Pennyless Pilgrimage*, published in 1630.

John Taylor was born of humble parents in Gloucester in 1580. He was educated at the local Grammar School and eventually was apprenticed to a London waterman. He later joined the Navy and saw much service in various parts of the world. Before 1603, he had made sixteen voyages in the Queen's ships and having been badly wounded in the leg, retired from the Navy in that year. He then became a Thames waterman.

In 1613 he was commissioned to arrange the details of a pageant on the River Thames—part of the marriage celebrations of Princess Elizabeth—daughter of James VI and I

(1567–1625)—and during this time met many of the important people of his day. Among these was John Erskine, Earl of Mar, and this resulted in his being invited to Scotland for the hunting season. Accordingly, in 1618, "John Taylor, The Kings Maiesties Water-poet" undertook his *Pennyless Pilgrimage* to Deeside.

Taylor left London on 14th July 'the sign being in Virgo, the moone foure dayes old, the wind at west'—and this was long before the publication of horoscopes in the daily Press! He took no money with him on the journey but his 'knapsake' was filled to capacity with the necessities of life including 'aquavita'. He records that a "gelded nagge bore his bagge" while he travelled on foot 'thumbing a lift' whenever opportunity presented itself. He reached Edinburgh on 13th August and proceeded to "a towne called Breekin (Brechin)" and from there via Glenesk, crossed the Fir Mounth Pass into Deeside. It is interesting to note that John Taylor's journey from Glenesk to Deeside was repeated in reverse two centuries later by Queen Victoria (1837–1901) who also left a record of the trip in her *Journal of Our Life in the Highlands*, published in 1868.

Curiously enough, many of Taylor's comments on Deeside, although couched in the quaint language of the time, seem quite topical. The weather, for example, came in for some caustic comment as the poet crossed the Fir Mounth Pass—"my teeth beganne to dance in my head with cold, like the Virginils jacks; and withal, a most familiar mist embraced me round, that I could not see thrice my length any way; withal, it yielded too friendly a deaw, that it did moysten throw my clothes: where the old Proverbe of a Scottish miste was verified, in wetting me to the skinne". The insects he encountered also appear to have annoyed the 'Water-poet' for he records that when he had "sup'd and went to bed, where I had not lain long, but I was forced to rise, I was so stung with Irish musketaes, a creature that had 6 legs".

However, despite the many hardships he endured, John Taylor eventually arrived at Braemar Castle where he rested in preparation for the real purpose of his visit—the great hunt. His narrative continues—"My good Lord of Marr having put me into that shape, I rode with him from his house, where I saw the ruines of an old Castle called the Castle of Kindroghit. It was built by King Malcolm Canmore (for a hunting house) who reigned in Scotland when Edward the Confessor, Harold, and the Norman William reigned in England: I speake of it, because it was the last House that I saw in those parts; for I was the space of twelve days after, before I saw either House, Comefield, or Habitation for any creature but Deere, wilde Horses, Wolves, and such like creatures, which made me doubt that I should never have seen a house againe".

"Thus the first day wee traveld eight miles, where there were small cottages built on purpose to Lodge in, which they call Longuhards, I thanke my good Lord Erskin, hee commanded that I should always bee lodged in his lodging, the kitchen being alwayes on the side of a banke, many Kettles and Pots boyling, and many spits turning and winding with great variety of cheere as Venison bak't, Sodden, rost and stu'de beefe, mutton, goates, kid, Hares, fresh salmon, Pidgeons, Hens, Capon, Chickens, Partridge, Moorcoots, Heathcocks, Caper-kellies, and Termagants; good Ale, Sacke, White, and Claret, Tent, (or Allegont) with most potent Aquavitae."

"All these, and more than these we had continually, in super-flous abundance, caught by Falconers, Fowlers, Fichers, and brought by my Lords Tenants and purveyors to victuall our Campe, which consisteth of fourteen or fifteen hundred men and horses."

John Taylor obviously enjoyed the great hunt—

"Through heather, moss, mongst frogs, and bogs and
fogs,
Mongst craggy cliffes, and thunder battered hills."

PLATE 19

Provost Ross's House and its neighbour 48–50 Shiprow, Aberdeen.

PLATE 20

(a) Silver medallion struck in honour of Archbishop William de Scheveze.

(b) Signature of Archbishop William de Scheveze on one of his books.

He tells that "in a space of two houres, forescore fat Deere were slaine". It would appear, however, that the hunt increased the appetite, for the poet continues—"Being come to our lodgings, there was such Baking, Boyling, Roasting, and Stewing . . . and after supper a fire of Fire-wood as high as an indifferent may-pole."

The great hunt lasted for the best part of a month moving from place to place—into Badenoch, to Darnaway Castle, Bog o' Gight (Gordon Castle), Huntly and back to Deeside.

John Taylor records that his return journey from Deeside was made by the 'Carry mount' (Cairn a' Mount) to Brechin where, quite exhausted, he stayed the night at the local inn. However, his adventures were by no means over. He had just climbed into his press-bed and was sound asleep when "a wench that was borne deafe and dumb came into his chamber at midnight—I being asleep—and she opened the bed, and would faine have lodged with me—the great travell over the mountains had tamed me; or if not her beauty could never have moved me". Startled out of his deep sleep, Taylor recounts that he "thrust my dumb heart out of my chamber and staked up my doore with a great chair". Next morning the 'Water-poet' complained to the inn-keeper about his nocturnal visitor and was asked to overlook the unfortunate incident as he quaintly records—"the wench had recently changed her maiden-head for the price of a Bastard not long before".

From Brechin, Taylor proceeded to Forfar, Dundee, Kinghorn, Burntisland and Edinburgh arriving in London on 10th October.

During the great plague of 1625 John Taylor evacuated to Oxford for safety and lodged at Oriel College. Eventually he became landlord of the well-known London inn *The Crown* which he re-named *The Ship* and died there in 1653 survived by his wife Alice who died four years later.

16

Kind Hearts and Coronets

"The remembrance of the past is the teacher of the future."

The dignified 18th-century dwelling-house—presently numbered 61 Schoolhill, Aberdeen—is passed by many people every day but few are aware of its existence. This is not surprising for the recessed position of the building on the south side of the street, wedged between the bulk of the old Central School (Aberdeen Academy) on the west, and a block of flats and shops on the east, adds to its obscurity. However, its architectural merits have long been familiar to the few interested in such matters.

The house is built of hand-dressed granite ashlar, probably from Rubislaw Quarries, with alternate window jambs of a darker stone which might have come from any one of several neighbouring granite quarries. The introduction of this darker stone adds interest to the design. The fenestration of the Schoolhill frontage is quite charming and is enhanced by the well-proportioned entrance doorway with its finely moulded architrave. Although down the years the interior of the house had been altered many times, it still retains several items of architectural interest, notably the staircase and the coved plaster ceilings on the first floor. Unfortunately, the name of the designer of No 61 Schoolhill is unknown, but it would appear from the general character of the house that it might well be the work of William Law, architect—designer of the Marischal Street bridge spanning Virginia Street—who was engaged in a number of buildings in the city at the time. Built in 1769 as a family house, No 61 has a fascinating story for its various owners were, in their several spheres of activity, unusually interesting people.

The land on which No 61 Schoolhill was subsequently built was originally called the Fore Croft, an area roughly triangular in form, bounded on the north by Schoolhill, on the west by the Denburn, and on the east by Fidies Wynd (later re-named Back Wynd) which, before the formation of Union Street, led from the Green to Schoolhill. Whether the Fore Croft was eventually re-named or broken up into sections and these were named separately, is uncertain, but about the middle of the 18th century when the first feus were taken on the south side of Schoolhill, the name Caberston Croft makes its appearance. At this time, Caberston Croft was the property of Marischal College.

Accordingly, in 1769, a charter was drawn up by Principal George Campbell and the Professors of Marischal College, granting permission to James Dun, Rector of the Grammar School, to erect a dwelling-house for his own occupation on Caberston Croft fronting the Schoolhill, the feu-duty being fixed at 15/6d. and $1\frac{1}{2}$ bolls of meal. Confirmation was given the following year when the house was completed. Nine years later Dun obtained a second charter granting him the right to form a side access to the garden ground at the rear of his property. It is interesting to note that Principal George Campbell himself took the adjacent feu—to the east of Dun's—on which he subsequently built a dwellinghouse and died there in 1796.

James Dun was born about the year 1708. His father, John Dun, was a wealthy merchant burgess in Campvere—related to the Dun family of Tarty in Logie Buchan, Aberdeenshire, but the exact relationship has never been established. James graduated M.A. at Marischal College at the age of twenty-four, an unusually advanced age for graduation in those days, but was immediately appointed Under Master at the Grammar School.

In 1744 he became Rector—an appointment for life, carrying with it the full salary 'during his lifetime'. This was altogether a happy arrangement for the Rector who lived until he was ninety. However, Dun retired from active teaching when he was eighty-three but continued as Rector, and although he could claim Lord Byron as his pupil, the poet was denied the honour of being taught by him. In 1772, in 'proof and testimony of their regard' the Senatus of Marischal College conferred on Dun an LL.D.

There seems little doubt that James Dun's good fortune in his appointments and remuneration was due to the *Dun Mortification* made to the Grammar School in 1631 by his kinsman Patrick Dun of Tarty, Doctor of Divinity and Principal of Marischal College. Patrick Dun bequeathed the entire Lands of Ferryhill to the School but unfortunately this valuable gift was frittered away by a succession of incompetent Magistrates otherwise the Grammar would have been one of the wealthiest schools in the country today.

James Dun would seem to have moved into his Schoolhill house about the year 1770—a convenient arrangement, for it stood almost opposite the Grammar School which had been reconstructed in 1757. The Rector's family consisted of his wife, Mary Beaton, and their daughter Mary who in 1767 married a master at the School—Dr James Beattie, famous as the author of *'The Minstrel'*. The Beatties lived with the Rector at No 61 Schoolhill. The Rector's wife died in 1781 and James Dun in 1789. The Beatties continued to live in the Schoolhill house until Dr Beattie's death in 1803 when the property was sold by Dr Dun's trustees to Peter Farquharson, advocate.

Peter Farquharson was the son of William Farquharson M.D. and his wife Margaret Souper. They claimed descent from one of Jacobite Branches of the Farquharson family of

Invercauld. Peter was born in Dundee. He subsequently moved to Aberdeen and graduated M.A. at Marischal College. In due course he set up in business as an advocate in Aberdeen where he built up a large county connection. Peter Farquharson purchased the estate of Abercattie in the parish of Tough, Aberdeenshire, but changed its name to Whitehouse. He died in 1855. It is uncertain whether Farquharson purchased No 61 Schoolhill with the intention of living there, or simply as a speculation. At all events, in a matter of months he sold the property to the Hon Alexander Duff.

The new owner of No 61 Schoolhill—the Hon Alexander Duff—was the third son and fifth child of William Duff, 1st Earl of Fife, by his second wife Jean Grant, eldest daughter of Sir James Grant of that Ilk. He was born at Rothiemay House in the year 1731 and received his early education at home along with his elder brother James—the minister of Rothiemay acting as their tutor. Being a younger son there seemed little chance of his ever succeeding to the title and it was considered best he should make his own way in life. Accordingly, he went to St Andrews University where he studied Law, eventually settling in Aberdeen where he began practising as an advocate. Duff appears to have specialised in estate work—the aftermath of Jacobite Rising of 1745 proving to be a lucrative source of revenue. Although he travelled a good deal, most of Duff's life was spent in Aberdeen.

In 1775 Alexander Duff married Mary Skene, eldest daughter of George Skene of that Ilk, and by her had a family of seven—three sons and four daughters. It was through this union that the Aberdeenshire estate of Skene eventually passed to the Fifes.

By the time Alexander Duff moved into No 61 Schoolhill, his family were grown up. His two elder boys—Sandy and Jamie—had been taken in hand by their uncle James, 2nd Earl of Fife, who sent them to Inchdrewer near Banff where a Dr

Chapman ran a highly esteemed boys' school. From Inchdrewer, Jamie went first to Westminster School, London, then to Christchurch, Oxford, and in 1794 to Lincoln's Inn to study Law. However, in 1796 he gave up his studies and joined the Army on the Continent. He returned to this country two years later and in 1799 married Maria Caroline, second daughter of John Manners and his wife Lady Louisa Tellemache, later Countess of Dysart. Unfortunately, their married life was lamentably short for Maria died in Edinburgh of hydrophobia in 1805—the year in which the Duffs moved into No 61 Schoolhill. On his father's death in 1811, Jamie succeeded as 4th Earl of Fife and on his return from active service abroad in 1833 took up permanent residence at Duff House, near Banff. He died there in 1857.

On leaving Inchdrewer, Sandy the second son, entered the Army as Ensign in the 65th Berkshire Regiment of Foot. He had a brilliant military career and in 1834 was knighted by William IV (1820–1837). Sandy—General Sir Alexander Duff—had inherited no estate and lived at Delgaty Castle near Turriff, where he died in 1851. George, the third son of Alexander Duff, died of an accident when two years of age.

Of Alexander Duff's four daughters—Jane married Major Alexander Francis Tayler of the Foot Regiment; Ann married Richard Wharton Duff of Orton in Elginshire; Sarah married Daniel Collyer of Wroxham in Norfolk, while Mary died young.

Alexander Duff's wife, Mary Skene, died in 1790—before he moved into No 61 Schoolhill—and ten years later, on the death of his brother James, Alexander succeeded as 3rd Earl of Fife. It would appear that Alexander's daughters—Jane and Ann—acted in turn as hostesses at No 61 and on their father's death in 1811 the Schoolhill property passed to them together with the sum of £4,000 to each by a bond of provision executed by Duff in 1801.

It has been said that Alexander Duff, 3rd Earl of Fife, was one of the few Duffs who was really musical and he played the violin extremely well, and one can picture the musical evenings in the elegant drawing room on the first floor of No 61 presided over by his Lordship—a genial host who enjoyed life. His letters from Aberdeen to his brothers make interesting reading and give a fascinating picture of life in the 18th-century burgh—"the town is tolerably gay just now, we have an Assembly once a fortnight and a Concert once a week, and a good deal of feasting". . . . "I am informed that the Duchess of Gordon intends to reside at Aberdeen some time this winter, they say she comes along with the North fencibles, who are to replace Lord MacDonald's Regt now at Aberdeen. If that is true the town will be more gay as her Grace likes to create amusement wherever she is." It would be interesting to know what 'amusement' Duchess Jean (Maxwell) had in mind for the douce Aberdonians. Of the Aberdeen climate, Alexander Duff had something to say—"the cold rages here most violently".

Alexander Duff died in April, 1811, at Duff House, and No 61 Schoolhill passed to his daughters Jane and Ann. In 1813, however, they disposed of the property to John Gordon of Craigmyle and his wife Mary Leslie.

John Gordon of Craigmyle was the only son of Richard Gordon, Advocate in Aberdeen—third son of John Gordon, 2nd of Seaton. Richard appears to have spent most of his life at Seaton House and was Procurator to the Town Council of Old Aberdeen—then an independent burgh. This office carried with it the salary of One Guinea a year, but in 1743 the Council felt it was an unnecessary expense and thereafter the post lapsed. In 1715 Richard Gordon was appointed Regent at King's College but two years later was deposed by Royal Commission—probably on account of his Jacobite sympathies. Richard was twice married, first to Elizabeth, daughter of John Leith of Leith-hall, and second to Mary Auchindachy by whom he had a son John. In 1742, Richard Gordon purchased the Lands of Craigmyle, near Torphins, from Alexander Farquharson of Monaltrie, and to this historic estate his son John succeeded on his father's death in 1763.

Of the new owner of No 61 Schoolhill—John Gordon of Craigmyle—little is known for he appears to have taken little part in public life. The Gordons appear to have spent most of their time at Craigmyle and in 1830 disposed of No 61 Schoolhill to Mrs Mary Henderson—the price paid for the property being £740. No 61 next passed to William Henderson M.D. when it became a doctor's house. Dr Henderson's trustees eventually disposed of the property and in 1884 it was acquired by the Aberdeen School Board. Thereafter, No 61 Schoolhill became the Janitor's Lodge for the Central School, erected in 1901, and subsequently it was converted into an annex of the school—by this time Aberdeen Academy. On the Academy's removal to Hazelhead, No 61 became vacant and on account of its situation and architectural merits was transferred by the Town Council of Aberdeen to the Art Gallery Committee. It is presently undergoing restoration and when completed will be used by the Gallery to house special collections of particular interest to the young.

17

A Royal Gambling Debt

"Here he lies where he longed to be;
Home is the sailor, home from sea"—R. L. Stevenson.

In a vault below the ancient parish church of Largo—that delightful little village between Leven and St Andrews—lie the bones of one who, had his legal claim to a royal gift been upheld, the Common Good Fund of Aberdeen, now worth over £1m. might never have come into being. This was Andrew Wood, 'father of Largo's sea-faring tradition'. He was born in the Kirkton of Largo, Fife, about the middle of the 15th century. Early in life, Wood went to sea and eventually became a prosperous merchant captain at the port of Leith.

It was during the reign of James III (1460–1488) that the Scottish Navy actually began to take definite form, for he was the first sovereign since Robert the Bruce (1306–1329) to appreciate the value of sea-power. The King considered an efficient fleet essential, but with the Scottish eye for economy, the ships he built or bought had to serve a double purpose—as merchantmen in times of peace and prosperity, and as fighting ships in the dark days of war. Consequently, the sea-captains of Fife and the Lothians, having received their royal commissions, formed a potent force against Scotland's enemies—notably the English.

Andrew Wood was one of those captains whose abilities and temperament fitted perfectly into the national requirements. He has indeed been called 'the Scottish Nelson' but this is perhaps an understatement for Wood had come to the top the hard way, was a 'bonnie fechter' who had bettered the pirates of many lands, and had trounced the English fleet on more than one occasion. Accordingly, in 1482—for these and many other services to Scotland—Andrew Wood was knighted on board his own ship by James III, and the following year the Lands of Largo, which he had previously held on lease, were granted to him by his grateful sovereign. Thereafter he became Sir Andrew Wood of Largo, Admiral of the Scottish Fleet, his flagship being the famous *Yellow Caravel*, a frigate of forty guns.

By this time, Sir Andrew had become a close friend of the King and they were much in each others' company, indeed in 1488 when James was obliged to flee from his rebel barons, it was Wood who came to his assistance, taking him on board ship and carrying him to safety across the Forth. Both the King and his Admiral were keen card-players—sometimes for pretty high stakes—and it is said that James was frequently in Wood's debt and royal I.O.Us were not infrequent.

The story now moves to Aberdeen—back to the 14th century and struggles of Robert the Bruce.

In the month of September, 1319, Robert the Bruce visited Aberdeen where he was no stranger. He was given a tremendous welcome by the citizens, many of whom were his former comrades-in-arms. It is obvious from the city's records that Bruce and his family had a strong affection for Aberdeen. They had first come to the burgh in 1306, weary, friendless and destitute, and had found shelter and loyal friends. By this time King Robert's daughter Matilda was married to Thomas Isaacs, the Town Clerk, so the family's ties with the burgh had become more personal. Well pleased with the reception he was given in Aberdeen and mindful of the help he had received in the past, King Robert granted a charter, gifting to the citizens in perpetual feu, his Royal Forest of Stocket—a hunting forest lying to the west of the burgh. This charter, which was given at Berwick on 10th December, 1319, is one of Aberdeen's greatest treasures.

The acquisition of the Stocket Forest brought responsibilities and in 1398 arrangements were made by the Magistrates for its protection and maintenance. Accordingly, foresters were appointed to guard the territory—what are now called the Freedom Lands—and it is interesting to note that the familiar name 'Foresterhill' derives from this 14th-century office.

For over a century the citizens of Aberdeen enjoyed the privileges of the Stocket Forest. However, in the year 1493, they were rudely shaken when it was announced that the late king—James III—had granted the Stocket Forest and the Castlehill of Aberdeen to his Admiral, Sir Andrew Wood of Largo, and that he intended sailing north to claim his gift.

The citizens were stunned. The provost, Alexander Reid of Pitfodels, was equal to the occasion. He called the citizens to meet him on the Heading Hill, explained the situation and to a man they determined to fight for their rights. In due course the gallant Admiral's flag-ship the *Yellow Caravel* was sighted off Girdleness but it would seem Sir Andrew either sensed opposition, or had been informed of it, so probably for the first time in his career, tactfully retreated.

But time was not to be lost and Provost Reid proceeded to Edinburgh carrying with him the proof of ownership—Bruce's charter of 1319—and on 20th June, 1494, Letters under the Great Seal of King James IV (1488–1513) were issued confirming the burgh's ownership of the Stocket Forest.

How did the situation arise? As mentioned before, James III was something of a gambler. Sir Andrew Wood was his most regular opponent and it is on record that the king was frequently in his admiral's debt. It is possible, therefore, that James's gift of the Stocket Forest and the Castlehill may have been in settlement of a gambling I.O.U. At all events, whatever the reason, the royal aberration had the Aberdonians worried.

Sir Andrew Wood retired to Largo Tower which he is said to have built about the year 1490 with a labour-force of

English, French and Portuguese—prisoners captured by him on his various voyages. The fragmentary ruins of his strong-hold stand within the grounds of Largo House, 'Sir Andrew's Tower' being a prominent feature. Another reminder of the Scottish admiral at Largo is 'Andrew Wood's Canal', a water-way said to have been constructed by him so that he might sail to Mass in Largo Kirk in his Admiral's Barge. The bed of this old water-way is still to be seen.

Andrew Wood married Elizabeth Lundy by whom he had two sons—Andrew, who succeeded to his father's estates which remained in the family until 1618, and John who eventually became secretary to the Regent Moray. Sir Andrew Wood died at Largo Tower in 1515. Tradition tells his last voyage was made by canal in his Admiral's Barge, manned by eight of his old crew, his battle-scarred pennon flying astern. He was buried in the family vault at Largo Kirk, his compass, cross-staff, sword and whistle with him. A plaque now marks the Scottish admiral's resting-place.

18

Provost Ross's House

*"Houses have distinct personalities either bequeathed
to them by their builders or tenants, absorbed from
their materials, or emanating from the general
environment."*—William Beebe.

Some twenty years ago, when the suggestion was made to
retain and restore Aberdeen's oldest dwelling—the building
now known as Provost Ross's House in the Shiprow—it
touched off one of the most bitter controversies the city had
known for many years. Looking back, it was an unsavoury
battle, waged with all the petty rancour of local party poli-
tics—a typical reaction when any attempt is made to preserve
the city's precious patrimony. However, the building was
eventually saved—though only by a few hours, a surreptitious
plot to pull it down having been outmanoeuvred. At all events,
it is the only building of architectural merit in the Shiprow today.

The story of the Shiprow—one of Aberdeen's oldest
streets—begins about the year 1290 when the burgh centre
moved from the Green to Castle Street. No doubt from a very
early period it had existed in the form of a footpath winding its
way round the base of St Katherine's Hill but by the 13th
century it had become a public thoroughfare called the
Shiprow—the *Vicus Navium* of the burgh's early charters.

Records show that the first houses to line the Shiprow were
timber-built structures with 'thackit' or 'divot' roofs—a
hazardous type of construction judging by the frequent out-
breaks of fire which, from time to time, devastated the town.

However, by the end of the 15th century the Shiprow had developed into being one of Aberdeen's most important and
elegant streets and retained its prestige for three cen-

turies—indeed until the formation of Marischal Street in 1768. Of course over the years the timber structures had gradually been replaced by stone-built houses, the homes of the important families whose names illuminate the city's annals, such as the Kennedys, Menzies, Chalmers and Davidsons.

A glimpse of everyday life in the Shiprow during the 16th century is gleaned from the Town Council's records of the time when preparations were being made for the visit of Margaret Tudor, Queen of James IV. According to custom, a 'clean up' was considered essential lest the pungent odours from the various closes, pends and vennels should assail the royal nostrils. Accordingly, the Town Council decreed that the 'pynouris'—the Shore Porters—should clear the 'hail toune of all myddings' while the citizens, especially those living in the Shiprow through which the Queen was to pass, were ordered to keep in close confinement for a fortnight prior to the royal visit, all swine usually at large in the street. For similar and perhaps more obvious reasons, horses were also banned from the Shiprow for a like period and as an added precaution house-holders were requested to deck their balconies and fore-stairs with fragrant evergreen boughs and sweet-smelling herbs.

However, in 1511, when Queen Margaret entered Aberdeen by the Shiprow Port and proceeded up the historic street, the site where Provost Ross's House now stands was occupied by one of the old timber dwellings built by the Menzies family about the year 1440. Eventually this property was acquired by Walter Brechin who, in 1591, disposed of it to Robert Watson—probably for its site value as no mention is made in the transaction of any building, only 'certaine landis on the wast syd of the Schipraw' valued at £20 Scots per annum. This Robert Watson, son of 'Maister Johnne Watsoune and his spouse Christian Collesone' is described as a 'wrycht'—house carpenter. In 1574 he had been admitted a trade burgess of Aberdeen and obviously had prospered.

At this time, Robert Watson's building associate was Andrew Jamesone 'maister measone', father of the celebrated portrait painter George Jamesone. In the latter part of the 16th century, Watson and Jamesone were frequently associated in various building projects in and around the burgh for both were highly-skilled craftsmen—such buildings as Jamesone's own house in the Schoolhill (1587) demolished in 1886, Mar's Castle in the Gallowgate (1595) demolished in 1897, Durris Castle (c. 1590), and of course Provost Ross's House (1593) built by Watson for his own occupation. As one might expect, all these houses had a strong 'family resemblance'.

The house Robert Watson built for himself conforms to the usual style of domestic street architecture of the period—rectangular in plan with two projecting rectangular towers front and back. Both towers are finished with simple, well-proportioned gables. The house is built of granite surface gatherings with dressed work of freestone and granite. Originally, the house was harled, except on the dressed work, while the roofs were of red pantiles. The Shiprow frontage has many interesting features notably the finely moulded eaves-course which on reaching the tower develops into a richly-carved corbel-table forming the projection from which the gable springs. The gables of the main house and towers are finished with plain skews, the 'peet-stanes' being carved with heraldic emblems and the date 1593. A 19th-century description of the property refers to carved freestone shields above the first floor windows facing the Shiprow but these have long since disappeared. Down the years and with its several owners, the internal planning arrangements of the house had been frequently altered consequently it is difficult to give any accurate indication of the original lay-out. However, even in its much altered state, it is obvious the building was planned with such elegance and comfort as was known at the time—the home of a prosperous Aberdeen burgess.

How long Robert Watson—the builder of the house—remained in occupation is uncertain but he was eventually succeeded in ownership by Alexander Farquhar, merchant burgess of the burgh. Farquhar was related to the families of Tonley and Mounie and was kinsman to Sir Robert Farquhar, Provost of Aberdeen in 1644—and again in 1650 when he was knighted during the visit of Charles II. The provost was reputed to be one of the wealthiest men in Scotland.

Alexander Farquhar's daughter Margaret succeeded to the property. She married Robert Skene, elder son of Andrew Skene of Ruthrieston and Pitmuxton and his wife Christian Skene of Overdyce, and the daughter of this union inherited the Shiprow house which eventually passed to her husband James Sinclair, younger of Seba. Sinclair sold the property to James Nicolson of Tarbrown, sometime Dean of Guild of Edinburgh, who in 1702 disposed of the house to John Ross of Clochcan and Arnage.

Ross was the second son of John Ross of Clochcan in the parish of Old Deer, by his wife Christian, daughter of Andrew Howieson, merchant burgess of Aberdeen. The family were cadets of Auchlossin who in turn were descended from the Roses of Kilravock. John was born in 1665 and at an early age became a merchant, trading chiefly with Holland, Amsterdam becoming his headquarters. In 1710 he was elected Provost of Aberdeen. In addition to Clochcan which he inherited from his father, Ross acquired the barony of Arnage in Ellon, Colp and Foresterhill. He made a considerable fortune trading with the continent and died in Amsterdam in 1714 where he was buried in the English Church. His widow survived him for many years living in the Shiprow house which today bears the provost's name while his armorial bearings are displayed over the old entrance doorway on the north side of the tower facing up the Shiprow.

By the end of the 18th century the Shiprow had begun to

decline. Its heyday as a residential area had passed for the well-known families had moved to the new and more fashionable quarters of the town. The old house deteriorated rapidly as it passed from one owner to another. Eventually, along with the neighbouring property No 48–50 Shiprow, it was acquired by Associated British Cinemas Ltd and in due course the two buildings—by this time quite derelict—passed into the safe-keeping of the National Trust for Scotland. A scheme was launched for their restoration and in September 1954, Provost Ross's House and No 48–50 Shiprow—by this time cleverly conjoined as an architectural group of unusual interest and charm—was opened by the Secretary of State for Scotland.

With the opening of the restored buildings and the eulogies made during the ceremony, it was felt by some that the policy of demolition which has wrought such havoc in Aberdeen was a thing of the past. Little wonder, they heard of 'a city that has learned to cherish such things' and of the stimulation engendered by the restoration 'to bring better order and more grace to our streets and buildings'. Noble sentiments these, but the question of the retention of Crimmonmogate's House, the Wallace Tower, Queen Street and the New Market was in the future.

19

A Rector's Family

*"Death comes to the monumental stones
And the names inscribed thereon."*—Ausonius.

Just within the southern boundary of Buchan, on the left bank
of the River Ythan and almost equidistant from the villages of
Ellon, Methlick and Tarves, lies the ancient barony of
Schivas—or Scheveze, to use the first spelling of the name.

The barony originally belonged to a family taking its name
from the place but when the Scheveze family settled in Buchan
is not recorded. The first member of the family to be noted is
Andrew de Scheveze—sometimes spelt 'Syves'—who held the
office of Vicar of Bervie in the Mearns. Little is known about
Andrew de Scheveze except that, towards the end of the 14th
century, he was appointed Rector of Aberdeen Grammar
School. The second recorded Rector of the School, Andrew de
Scheveze died *circa* 1418 when he was succeeded by John
Homyll.

About eight years after the death of Andrew de Scheveze,
another member of the family is mentioned. This is John de
Scheveze who, in 1426, is styled 'Clerk to King James I.' It has
been suggested that John, the Clerk, was a younger brother of
Andrew, the Rector, but there is no confirmation for this.

The most outstanding member of the Scheveze family was
William. He was educated at Louvain under Spiricus the astrol-
oger and made such progress in medicine and theology that he
was without equal in Britain or France. It is believed that
Andrew was a son of John, the Clerk, and if this assumption is
correct, he was a nephew to Andrew, the Rector. The exact

relationship between these three members of the family has never been established but it seems certain they were closely related.

By the middle of the 15th century, William de Scheveze had become one of the chief advisers to James III (1460–1488) who frequently sent him as Ambassador to foreign countries. That Scheveze exercised considerable influence over the king there is little doubt but the suggestion made by his contemporaries that his power over James was due to his 'scheming and astrological quakery' is not borne out by the facts for Scheveze was a man of considerable abilities and learning.

In 1478 William de Scheveze was created second Archbishop of St Andrews. Shortly after his elevation to the Arch-episcopate, Scheveze made a pilgrimage to the Mearns where he visited the celebrated Shrine of St Palladius near Fordoun. There, the Archbishop carried out extensive alterations to the Chapel of St Palladius and caused a silver casket to be made for the reception of the Saint's relics. The particular interest shown by Archbishop Scheveze in the Fordoun Shrine may not be unconnected with the fact that his kinsman—perhaps uncle—the Grammar School Rector, had been vicar of Bervie, near Fordoun, some seventy years before.

William de Scheveze has been described as an 'ambitious and worldly churchman of the type of Wolsey'. Whether this is just criticism it is now impossible to say, but his physical resemblance to the Cardinal is quite remarkable. William de Scheveze died in the year 1497 and was interred in the Cathedral of St Andrews. To Scheveze, St Andrews University owes the nucleus of its Library, for the Archbishop was a great lover and collector of books. Several of his books can be seen in the Library at King's College, Old Aberdeen, a number of them bearing his elaborate signature, as elegant and decorative as any piece of mediaeval illumination.

The Scheveze family exercised considerable influence in

north-east Scotland during the 15th century but as the century closed, the main line—Scheveze of that Ilk—terminated through an heiress of Scheveze marrying a Lipp which carried the barony to that family. A cadet branch appears to have settled in Aberdeen where, in 1597, an Archibald Scheveze became a Burgess of Guild. Another branch settled in Inverness establishing themselves at Muirtown—Robert Scheveze of Muirtown being one of the chief witnesses at the trial of Simon, Lord Lovat, in 1746.

From that time onwards, the influence of the family appears to have been on the wane. Apart from the beautiful silver medal struck in honour of Archbishop William de Scheveze in 1491—now in the National Museum of Antiquities, Edinburgh—and of course his books, it would appear that nothing has survived of the family but their name, while Aberdeen Grammar School itself, a seminary of international reputation when Andrew de Scheveze was its Rector six hundred years ago, has in our time, passed—or more correctly, has been pushed—into history so that today—

"Nocht remains bot faime."

Index of principal Names

Index of principal Places